POND PASSION TO PROFIT

Achieving Prosperity and Fulfilment in the Business of Water Features

Mark Wilson

Pond Passion to Profit
Achieving Prosperity and Fulfilment in the Business of Water Features
© 2024 Mark Wilson

All rights reserved. No part of this book may be reproduced, stored in a retrieval system, or transmitted in any form or by any means (electronic, mechanical, photocopy, recording, scanning, or other) except for brief quotations in critical reviews or articles without the publisher's prior written permission.

ISBN: 9781068711107 Paperback

Published by: Inspired By Publishing

The strategies in this book are presented primarily for your enjoyment and educational purposes. Every effort has been made to trace copyright holders and obtain their permission to use copyright material.

The information and resources provided in this book are not just theoretical, but are based on the author's extensive personal experiences in the business of water features. Any outcome, income statements, or other results are based on the author's experiences, and there is no guarantee that your experience will be the same. There is an inherent risk in any business enterprise or activity, and there is no guarantee that you will have results similar to the author's from reading this book.

The author reserves the right to make changes and assumes no responsibility or liability whatsoever on behalf of any purchaser or reader of these materials.

For additional resources and companion services that guide and support you through your journey, we invite you to visit https://mark.thepondadvisor.co.uk/business.html

CONTENTS

Introduction 1

Part 1: Foundations of Success 9
   1. The Pond Professional's Mindset 11
   2. Understanding The Pond Industry 29

Part 2: Crafting Your Unique Offer 49
   3. Designing with Creativity 51
   4. Building with Excellence 69
   5. Maintenance Mastery 85

Part 3: Growing Your Business 103
   6. A Guide to Building Your Brand 105
   7. Sales Techniques and Customer Relationships ... 127
   8. Project Management and Operations 151

Part 4: Maximising Profit and Impact 179
   9. Financial Strategies 181
   10. Expanding Your Business 203

Part 5: Building a Legacy 223
   11. The Future of Your Pond Business 225
   12. Creating a Business That Matters 243

Conclusion: Your Roadmap to Success 255

INTRODUCTION

Do you dream of creating a water feature business that will support you and your loved ones and bring you pride and satisfaction?

You may have started your business but are still not making the money or having the freedom or professional joy you thought you would by now.

If you've picked up this book, you may envision building a business that will stand the test of time and bring you the life you have always dreamed of. However, you may be unsure of how to get there or looking for some golden nuggets.

Whatever your situation, I'm glad this book has found its way into your hands. I want to help you navigate your path to expanding your business or finding your dream role by avoiding common pitfalls and accelerating your success. Along the way, I will also guide you in building a business that matters—not just to you but to everyone it touches. From establishing a solid foundation to exploring innovative expansion strategies, you'll learn how to create a lasting legacy.

A business in the water feature industry offers incredible freedom and responsibility. This niche market presents a unique opportunity to blend creativity with entrepreneurship, tapping into a growing trend towards personal and community wellness spaces. As more individuals seek sanctuary in their surroundings amidst a fast-paced world, the demand for tranquil garden water features has surged. These installations enhance property value and support environmental sustainability through water conservation and habitat creation.

The most exciting aspect of the water feature industry is its ability to reconnect people with nature. Water features create serene spaces that encourage relaxation, healing, and enjoyment of the simple pleasures in life. They attract birds, dragonflies, and other wildlife, turning gardens into vibrant ecosystems. Aquatic entrepreneurs can lead the market in people's gardens with advancements in eco-friendly technologies and sustainable materials.

Additionally, the rise of smart home integration allows for beautiful and intelligently managed water features, making them more appealing to tech-savvy clientele. This is the perfect time to channel your passion for nature and design into a profitable venture that brings beauty and peace to people's lives.

So how do we get there?

When I left employment and started my business over 20 years ago, I only wanted to make money and not be told what to do. I didn't have a detailed plan; I just had a burning desire to do things my way. But in the first 10 years of my business, I often felt isolated. One demanding customer had made my life miserable, and I had no one to blame but myself. I was trying to please everyone instead of trusting my instincts and charging enough to cover my expenses. Everyone, including myself, thought I was strange (yes, I am still pond-crazy, but I have found others like me).

Back then, I still needed to learn how to build a business. I was still creating a glorified job, not letting go of the handrails, calling it a business. I loved it then and was good at it (this was my passion, and I was still in my comfort zone). But passion alone isn't enough to sustain a business.

It took physical injury (hurting my back by consistently trying to do all the work myself) to finally shift things for me. I was forced to look at my garden water feature business with a fine-toothed comb and highlight areas I could do with help. I hired three full-time guys to be my arms and legs. With my oversight, the service side of my business improved. As I learned to delegate and trust more, the business started surviving without my constant presence on the job site or even having to make sales calls.

My business has grown exponentially, transforming from a modest setup in my bedroom and garage to a vibrant facility with adult-sized sandboxes for training the next generation, a display centre, and half an acre of water feature gardens. Today, we boast nearly a million in inventory and expansive yard space. I've fully stepped away from the job sites to focus on marketing and fostering a positive company culture, demonstrating how much we've expanded from our humble beginnings as a one-man operation.

The growth of the business has brought profound improvements to my personal life. My back pain, a constant companion in the early days, has vanished thanks to regular Chiropractic care, and I no longer rely on painkillers. This physical relief has allowed me to pursue my lifelong ambitions, including travelling to Japan twice to select dream koi for my "Koi Palace." These experiences have not only fulfilled personal dreams but also enhanced the quality and diversity of our offerings.

Most importantly, I've found a balance that many entrepreneurs strive for. My life no longer revolves around work in the traditional sense; instead, I get to play and engage in what's most important to me. Financially, we are nearing a significant milestone with our house nearly paid off and our debts almost cleared, setting a solid foundation for future freedom and security. This stability has allowed me to live a fulfilled life where work and play blend seamlessly, and I am living my dream.

But looking back to when I first started, I can see exactly where I went wrong. Let me tell you, I wish I had this damn book back then. I don't want burnout or damage (whether to you, your business or your personal life) to be the reason things finally shift for you. I want to help you address potential pitfalls before they threaten to happen so that you can live your dream, too.

I know that running a business can be daunting for most. However, following the steps I have laid out in this book will make it much more manageable. I made the mistakes so that you don't have to.

My lifelong passion for freshwater water features has shaped my entrepreneurial spirit, leading me to want to find ways to earn money to play in the garden. Perhaps you are the same. In this book, I will guide you to achieve just that. After all, the more money you make, the bigger the pond you can create.

Let's Dream, Plan and Enjoy, but first, I need to be straightforward with you: I don't have a magic wand. This book doesn't offer quick fixes or a promise of effortless riches. Will you make mistakes? Yes. Hopefully, you will learn from them. This book is not for you if you want to make money without doing the work. This book is for aspiring aquatic entrepreneurs eager to build sustainable, impactful businesses that achieve financial success and, as a result, contribute positively to the world.

This book covers everything from the pond professional's mindset and the principles of aquatic art to ensuring longevity, maximising profit, and, ultimately, building a legacy. How you consume the information and use it is totally up to you. Whether you want to read the book as I designed it from point A to point B or jump around to different chapters, it's up to you. The main goal is to make enough money to do what you want for as long as possible.

Imagine seeing your business grow and evolve with new clients who know who you are and want to work with you and no one else.

Your journey starts here—with every page you turn and every strategy you implement. Build the business you've always dreamed of, and enjoy the process. Let's build something remarkable together and ripple the passion for water features into lasting success and fulfilment. Everything starts with a ripple!

"Strategy and Discipline = Success"

PART 1: FOUNDATIONS OF SUCCESS

"The only limit to our realisation of tomorrow is our doubts of today."
- Franklin D. Roosevelt

1
THE POND PROFESSIONAL'S MINDSET

The pond industry offers a rewarding career that requires a passion for work, creativity, and innovation. A successful pond professional commits to continuous learning, professionalism, and quality to stay at the forefront of the industry. So, finding your "why" is essential in fueling passion and motivation. Performance, passion, and purpose are crucial to success in any business, including those related to garden water features.

The pond industry is a close-knit community that fosters growth and appreciation for the craft. Its flexibility and fulfilment potential are unparalleled, allowing for personal satisfaction and professional autonomy.

Expertise transcends skill, requiring a deep knowledge of one's niche.

It all starts with your attitude and approach to your business. In this chapter, I provide practical tools for implementing an approach that prioritises sustainability, fulfilment, and impact.

Performance

Starting with performance emphasises its importance; anything you want to achieve starts with this. Your performance at work or in your personal life is the key to the success of the outcome you wish to bring to the world. It should be no different working on your passion project or whether you're working for someone else.

For example, if you're sweeping a patio, your performance is indicated by effort, energy, and enthusiasm for what you're doing. On a job site, it's easy to spot who the owners are. I'm not talking about the business owner. I'm talking about the project owners who own that particular task. We have all seen people pushing stuff around; you know that they do not own it like a boss. Their energy, effort, and enthusiasm tell you they don't want to be doing the task. They may be doing enough to fill in their time sheet with enough performance not to get removed from the job.

On the other hand, we have seen people giving the task the white glove treatment, doing their best and testing if it's up to the standard. I have experienced my helpers sweeping up the patio pavers and, on occasion, walking around the corner with the homeowner on the final walk-through to see them polishing the porcelain, thinking that's the standard. It is much better than finding them sitting around the van waiting to leave. They want that customer or the person they are doing the task for to see the correct level of performance.

If the task at hand needs a seven-star service, that is the level it needs to be. I always watch my performance, even when writing this book. I follow a practice run in my mind. I want my reader or client to experience first-hand what I am trying to achieve without distractions.

When my customer or one of my customer's friends comes around the corner to see us or what we are doing, they are not distracted by the waste on the patio or tread on that single piece of gravel on the lawn. I even go as far as to put everything back in its place if we move something (sometimes referring to a before picture). Many contractors and other tradespeople comment on the level of detail we provide. We go as far as combing the grass after we lift the boards, which have been down for a couple of days (with a lawn rake, not a pocket comb, I must add).

How do you think a customer will feel when they come round the corner and see you doing something in their garden that they wouldn't even do themselves? You or your team need to go the extra mile so your customer feels the need to say something about your performance. It could be, "Don't worry about that", and you raise the bar and reply, "It's our pleasure". In my business, most of our clients become our friends; we go the extra mile, break bread together, and want to spend time in their garden. They don't want us to leave.

The last 10%, or the detail, is what people always remember, and this is what you need to focus on. It's about more than just getting the feature finished on time. It's about going the extra mile and putting in your soul or stamp on that one-of-a-kind custom creation, plus making and sending out the right ripples.

Last but not least is efficiency:

Are you performing efficiently?
Are you doing the job to the best of your ability?
Have you thought about what you are doing?
Is there a better way?

Is there a more efficient way of doing this with the same or a better impact?

When you start a job, even if it's a small task in a client's garden, you need to foster the thought that you need to protect the area not only with the client in mind but for yourself and the speed of the job. We will cover up the grass, because nothing is worse than coming outside your house to look at your outstanding new water feature…and standing in a muddy mess. Nothing is worse than finding stuff you need to tidy up or paying someone to help you after contractors have finished, unless it was discussed before and planned.

I understand the weather conditions. You sometimes can't avoid mud everywhere, but it's quick and efficient to put stuff down and let your clients know it's potentially going to be a mess; they might not have had someone working on their property recently, or even better, they have, and you're better than the last company. If you are walking to the van to get a tool, think about what is on your feet.

Do I need to tidy up?
Do I need to protect the grass?

It's all about efficiency, and the customers appreciate that.

If you need to sweep outside the front of the house, do it, but do it better than before you showed up. Don't just brush things around and chuck a bucket of water over and think that's fine; that's how everyone does it. Think about your performance and efficiency, and keep that neat. But if you do, tidy up better than it was before you started.

If you're performing at your best, you think about all the different eventualities.

When you turn up to build a pond for a client, if you're going to be there for more than a couple of days, ask the client early on (even on your pre-job walk-through design consultation): "How are your neighbours?" They will tell you or give you an inclination if you have a problem with the neighbours. If they get on with the neighbours, don't cause them to start having problems. You want to ensure you meet the neighbour's expectations and avoid parking in the way or creating any mess.

Go above and beyond; it's even better to go out of your way to help the neighbours (they might want a pond at some point). They must enjoy you being around if it's beneficial or efficient to move over their property, even the slightest little bit, like a bottle of wine or card, to thank them. You can ask your clients for recommendations on what you can do for the neighbour. What is it in return for the hospitality? It goes a long way for you, your client, and the neighbour.

Practical Steps to Enhance Performance

- **Invest in training and development.**
  Continuously improve your skills and encourage those within your team to enhance performance and customer satisfaction.
- **Set clear objectives, like increasing customer satisfaction or Google reviews.**
  These improvement and efficiency objectives must be measurable, reducing project completion times (are you tracking how long things take?).
- **Assess your performance constantly.**
  Always look at your processes, identifying any bottlenecks and areas for improvement.

An outstanding performance comes from challenging yourself and being able to pursue your dreams. I might not know your name, but you have a dream. Let us make that dream come true.

Passion

Passion is the driving force behind the dedication to creating and maintaining beautiful, sustainable aquatic environments. When you have the same passion as someone else, people want to hang out with you; you can energise and inspire people, and positive, passionate people are infectious. I love it when I find people as passionate about garden water features as I am, and I love bringing people up, even for a split second, to the same level of passion I have, which you will surely get from reading this book.

What happens if you have too much passion for a project?

Suppose you are anything like me. You can and will get excited, so warn your potential customers. You don't want your passion to lead you to design a £50,000 water feature when the client's budget is £5,000.

Conversely, you don't want to be preparing a £5,000 feature if they want to dream more significant than your current comfort zone. You're wasting not only your time, but also their time. Your passion for what you do should fuel them. So I'm not saying don't share your enthusiasm, but warn your client before you go out that you get excited and would love to share your ideas for what to do with their garden space. You get excited; they get excited. But you want to know their level of investment before going out, because you can still get excited about a smaller budget.

Your passion is the driving force of your business. You can see the potential as soon as you go into a garden. It would help if you got this out of your head and into the homeowner's head, so they can get excited about what you see and what you can create in their back garden.

Your enthusiasm for aquatic design and ecology fuels innovation, inspires creative solutions, and motivates continuous learning and improvement. I am passionate about providing a suitable water feature for the right situation. Sometimes, customers think it needs to be done differently, and that's okay. We understand we can only be a good fit for some.

Practical Steps to Nurture Your Aquatic Passion

- **Remind yourself why you started!**
  The first and most important one is to remind yourself why you started this journey in the first place. Ask yourself what you love about ponds and water features. It might also be a business that sells water features. For 25 years, I was happy being a pond guy who happened to run a business. Then my body and mind said to stop. I became a business guy who happened to supply, build, and maintain ponds.

- **Stay engaged with industry events and networking opportunities.**

    Your passion for what you're doing and providing for others will help you stay the course when you hit technical difficulties, potential setbacks or market fluctuations. Suppose you are passionate about ponds, water features, and the general aquatics industry. Starting with the mindset, "How can I give?" means that when the time comes, you will have some help from within the industry that will help you overcome those obstacles, and sharing your passion within the industry will only lift the whole industry. A rising tide lifts all ships.

- **Pursue personal projects that allow you to explore your creativity and passion.**

    Next up is building or creating a water feature for yourself. It is fulfilling; some people must close themselves and live the lifestyle. That's okay if that's where you want to spend your money; many contractors own water features that would cost more than the homes they live in.

- **Surround yourself with other passionate individuals who share your enthusiasm for the pond industry.**

    Get around other people with the same passion. This might be an industry networking opportunity where you can keep up with the latest innovations and trends. Also, when you're struggling, the industry will pick you up. Other people will win, or you're all in the same boat.

I remember the saying, "Show me your friends, and I'll show you your future". It's so true; it will happen if you spend time with people you want to emulate, or have their internal thermostat set higher for the things you want to achieve.

I like to put analogies to things. Let's think for a second that you wanted to understand the feeling of jumping out of a plane, but you fear heights. If you surround yourself with the right people, you know that one day, you will find yourself on a plane, and they will also be helping you out of that plane. They will look after you, and you get such a sense of achievement when you pull that off. You should avoid repeating the experience, but you can do everything.

You can flip this to many things; use this to do something that scares you.

Purpose

What is your purpose? Purpose can be a profound question for some people. For others, it's easy.

I want to inspire people by highlighting garden water features, which are more than just an outside ornamental feature. Everything starts with a ripple. Some people must be shown or guided to a water feature for their lifestyle or path. They don't know why they like something, but they like it. I love everything freshwater. I can't pick just one thing about freshwater that makes me happier. It changes, and your experience changes.

For others, it might be family or providing for people you care about. One of my core values in life and business is "Doing things that matter, with people that matter, for people that matter".

A purpose-driven business in the pond industry focuses on creating value that extends beyond financial gain:

Environmental Impact
Your purpose could emphasise sustainable practices and water feature designs that support biodiversity, water conservation, and ecological health. Suppose you think about the watering hole. You might be thinking of a safari where everything is attracted to that water. Lots of animals need fresh water, and animals are attracted to garden ponds all over the world. You can double the wildlife in your garden with a pond (that can be seen) and double that amount again with the sound of water. Your purpose might be creating a place where new life can

emerge, and aquatic insects can thrive. Algae is the start of life as we know it. Ecosystems are enormous once you start going down that path.

Customer Experiences
We seek to enrich clients' lives through the beauty and tranquillity of our water features, enhancing their connection to nature and mental well-being.

Contribution to the Community
Helping people to dream of, plan, and enjoy ponds and water features has been one of my callings in life. I hope to positively impact the broader community through education and inspiration, conservation initiatives with rainwater harvesting, and public projects that promote environmental awareness and enjoyment of natural water features.

Success is different for a lot of people. If the reason you're doing what you're doing is enough, then you're successful. Don't let anyone else get in your way of pursuing success; it's a delicate balance, an ongoing process of growth and adaptation. Continuously strive to improve your performance, and this doesn't mean it all has to be about work. Your performance is also measured by your ability to recover, relax, and do what is needed. You're only sometimes lifting stones. You might have to work on yourself mentally, so you must put in more gardens and water features. Nurturing your love and living out your purpose will help you build a successful, rewarding, and impactful business.

Be bold (plant your flag), dream big (but don't beat yourself up), and take actionable steps based on the correct input to achieve the desired outcomes.

Think about this for a second: Would you continue running if you had to remove the finish line? That's an exciting thought. Would you even start running without the finish line? Is it about the destination, the reward, the journey, who you're spending time with, and what you do daily? This all comes down to your performance, your passion, and your purpose.

Practical Steps to Live Out Purpose
- Articulate your personal and your business's purpose beyond profit.
- Identify ways to integrate sustainable practices and designs into your water features.
- Develop programs or initiatives that contribute to the community, such as educational content or conservation efforts in schools and colleges.
- Communicate your purpose to your clients to build trust and loyalty.

What's next? Well, this is over to you.

- **Evaluate your current performance**
  Assess your quality of work, customer satisfaction, and operational efficiency. Identify areas for improvement and set actionable goals to enhance these KPIs (key performance indicators).
- **Reignite your passion**
  Remind yourself why you started and what you love about it. Seek new sources of inspiration, whether through industry events, networking, or personal projects, to keep your passion alive and well.
- **Define your purpose**
  Describe what you stand for beyond making money. Consider how you can make a difference in your community, contribute to environmental sustainability, or enhance your customers' lives meaningfully.

Reflecting on how you can align these three Ps is not a one-time task but an ongoing process of growth and adaptation. By continuously striving to improve your performance, nurture your passion, and live out your purpose, you'll build something bigger than you can imagine: successful but also rewarding and impactful. Encourage yourself to dream big, take actionable steps towards these goals, and remember that the journey towards aligning performance, passion, and purpose is as fulfilling as the destination itself.

In this chapter, we have covered how performance, passion, and purpose are not just strategies for success but three fundamental approaches that ensure sustainability, fulfilment, and impact.

We all have limited time, and we must use it wisely. Sometimes, taking risks can lead us to discover our passions, find our purpose, and perform at our best.

The biggest challenge we face regarding creativity and innovation is taking risks. However, it's essential to understand that the most significant risk in life is not taking one. To navigate this challenge, we must be willing to take calculated risks.

Becoming a successful water feature professional can be challenging, but viewing these challenges as opportunities for growth and learning is essential. Failure is an inevitable part of growth, and it's crucial to take the time to learn from mistakes and prevent similar issues in the future. Trust is the most valuable asset in the pond business, so building trust with clients by being transparent and delivering on promises is essential. Strong relationships with clients, suppliers, and peers are crucial, and attending industry events and collaborating on projects can provide support, inspiration, and opportunities for growth.

To achieve success, it's essential to define what success means to you, set achievable goals, and develop a plan to reach them. Finally, it's essential to stay flexible and be willing to adapt to changes in trends, client preferences, and environmental regulations to remain relevant and successful.

"Whether you think you can, or you think you can't – you're right."
- Henry Ford

2

UNDERSTANDING THE POND INDUSTRY

Ponds have been cherished throughout history, evolving from decorative basins in ancient civilisations. Egyptians incorporated ornamental ponds, pools, and irrigated gardens into their landscapes over 4,000 years ago, blending beauty with biodiversity. Initially symbols of luxury and power, modern ornamental garden ponds now focus on sustainability, creating natural habitats that support diverse wildlife, promoting water conservation with biological filtration, and offering serene landscapes for enjoyment and relaxation. This transition reflects a growing commitment to environmental stewardship and creating harmonious, functional ecosystems within gardens.

The Evolution of the Pond Industry

The pond industry has seen remarkable growth and transformation, driven by an increasing desire among homeowners to enhance their gardens. With more people valuing time spent at home, the trend of creating outdoor living spaces has surged, supported by the global availability of diverse landscaping products.

At our core, human desires are fundamentally simple: yearning for comfort, warmth, nourishment, and hydration. Beyond these basic needs, we are drawn to experiences enriching our lives, sensory engagement, and the calming influence of natural elements. Water meets these sensory needs through dynamic movement, soothing sounds, and reflective qualities. These enhancements beautify our surroundings and offer a peaceful haven that aligns with our natural affinity for water. The sound of flowing water, in particular, reduces stress and fosters well-being, making water a cherished addition to any garden.

Transforming outdoor spaces into extensions of our living areas is not only feasible but immensely gratifying. The emphasis on outdoor aesthetics and eco-friendly landscaping has become a priority for homeowners and businesses. In this landscape revolution, ponds and water features have taken centre stage, acting as communal hubs just like the warmth of a fire pit, where family and friends can gather and create lasting memories. Water features add a permanent visual allure to our gardens and come with profound environmental benefits. They serve as tranquil sanctuaries that soothe the soul, support local ecosystems, and enhance biodiversity, making them an invaluable addition to any outdoor space.

This industry's scope extends beyond mere aesthetics; it encompasses the creation of ecosystems that support local wildlife, improve air quality, and contribute to an individual's mental and physical well-being. The popularity of naturalistic water feature designs that mimic nature from a beauty and functionality point of view reflects a broader trend towards environmentally responsible landscaping. These approaches prioritise using native flora, biological filtration, and water-saving techniques, contributing to global biodiversity and combating climate change.

Technological advancements have also played a crucial role in the industry's growth, with innovations in filtration, intelligent colour-changing lights, and automatic dosing systems, making pond maintenance more efficient and user-friendly. As technology continues to evolve, pond professionals are equipped with tools that allow for more precise control over water quality, underwater lighting effects, and overall pond health, enhancing the user experience and expanding the possibilities for design and functionality.

The landscaping industry has shifted into niches over the years, with more and more people focusing on aquatics as their full-time profession. There are hundreds of companies in the UK specialising in outdoor water features and offering pond services. The UK has a strong gardening culture, and we have a range of businesses, from small solopreneurs (independent owner-operators) to larger landscaping firms. It offers comprehensive pond services, including design, garden water feature installation, maintenance and restoration, catering to a wide range of client needs and preferences.

As awareness of environmental issues grows and people seek refuge in their outdoor spaces, the pond industry is well-positioned for continued expansion. The demand for sustainable, beautiful water features that serve as aesthetic centrepieces and functional habitats is expected to drive innovation and growth in the industry for years.

Market Trends and Opportunities

Market trends reflect the dynamic currents steering the pond industry, shaped by evolving customer preferences, cutting-edge technological innovations, and shifts in regulatory landscapes. These trends are vital indicators of where consumer interests lie, from eco-friendly water features to intelligent, automated pond systems.

Staying abreast of these trends enables pond professionals to anticipate demands, adapt to new standards, and harness technology to offer sustainable, captivating outdoor spaces. Understanding market trends is vital to navigating the industry's future, ensuring businesses survive and thrive by meeting and exceeding the expectations of today's environmentally conscious and tech-savvy consumers.

Grasping market dynamics is crucial for strategically positioning your pond business and seizing new opportunities. It involves analysing how consumer preferences, competition, and economic conditions interact and influence the market. Understanding these dynamics allows you to anticipate trends, adapt your offerings, and innovate ahead of shifts, ensuring your business remains relevant and competitive. This knowledge will enable you to tailor your services to meet evolving demands, opening doors to growth and establishing your business as a leader in the pond industry.

Greg Wittstock, also known as "The Pond Guy," is an entrepreneur who has successfully capitalised on market trends to grow his pond business. His company, Aquascape Inc., became a leading innovator in North America's pond and water garden industry by introducing ecosystem ponds that are easier to maintain and more environmentally friendly than traditional designs. Wittstock's approach to educating consumers and contractors through seminars, online content, and television appearances has significantly shaped the industry's direction. He has also become a leading content creator, teaming up with customers, other creators, and celebrities to reach many people.

Trends in 2024 and Beyond

Naturalistic Pond Designs

Biophilic Design

Biophilic is a new buzzword in the industry. It means where we integrate nature into our spaces, prioritising well-being and sustainability. Biophilic designs are trending, especially in ponds and water features. Unlike traditional water features in the UK, this design fosters a deeper connection with the natural world, addressing growing demands for health (mental and physical health), environmental responsibility, and authentic nature experiences. Biophilic design connects us deeply with the environment. This approach increases demand for ponds and water features that mimic natural landscapes. Naturalistic designs incorporate native plants, rocks, and waterfalls to create habitats that attract wildlife and provide a serene retreat in one's garden.

Wildlife-Friendly Features

The trend towards wildlife-friendly water features, particularly still-water wildlife ponds, is driven by a desire to counter habitat loss and heighten environmental consciousness. These features aim to bolster biodiversity and sustainability by providing natural habitats for local wildlife, utilising zero-electricity solutions, and diverse plantings to support British wildlife conservation amidst diminishing natural spaces. Homeowners and businesses are increasing interest in establishing water features that nurture local biodiversity, including birds, amphibians, and beneficial insects. However, a note of caution: Stillwater ponds without filtration still require more active waste management by the owners. To address this, like many industry professionals, we advocate using wildlife-friendly filtration systems and moving water in sparkling wildlife ponds to combine ecological benefits with ease of maintenance.

Eco-Friendly Materials and Practices

Sustainable Materials

There's a growing preference for sustainably sourced or recycled materials, which reduce the environmental footprint of water feature construction. This includes using local stone, recycled plastics for decking, insect meal as the primary protein (instead of the standard fish meal) in fish foods, and other environmentally friendly building materials.

Rainwater Harvesting

Integrating rainwater harvesting systems with sustainable water features is becoming more common. But what about the mosquitoes? Recirculating rainwater with a water feature can stop mosquitoes and keep the water sweet. Ponds can also be filled and topped off, so remember to water the garden with your collected rainwater.

Chemical-Free Solutions

The demand for natural water treatment methods is increasing, and lots of money is being spent on improving our waterways, including biological and chemical filtration in the form of radiation (UV light), water plants that naturally purify water, and the introduction of beneficial bacteria, which are preferred over harsh chemical treatments. Several British water plants have endemic bacteria living solely on their root structure within the water column. Some water plants can even remove heavy metals and other toxins from water. These methods enhance water quality in an eco-friendly manner and create healthier environments for fish and plants.

Smart Pond Technology

Automated Dosing Systems

Innovative automated dosing systems regulate the addition of water treatments, such as conditioners and nutrients, ensuring the health and balance of pond ecosystems. Programmable and controllable via smart devices, these systems simplify maintenance. Some advanced units automatically adjust dosages based on real-time water quality data, reducing the need for frequent manual testing and adjustments. Look after the water, and the aquatic life (including the fish) will look after themselves.

Automated Maintenance Systems

Technology for monitoring and maintaining water quality, such as smart filters and UV clarifiers, can now be controlled via smartphone apps. This allows for easier management of pond ecosystems and ensures optimal conditions with minimal manual intervention. Some people, however, are turned off by all of this advancing technology. I prefer to keep things simple, with a mechanical filter on one side and a biological filter on the other. I only add something wet if I have to, including new pond fish (this all comes from a biosecurity point of view, drying nets and maintenance equipment as needed).

Understanding your water feature is critical; if you prefer natural approaches that don't require too much attention or rely on constantly cleaning the system, that's okay.

LED Lighting and Energy Efficiency

Advances in LED technology provide energy-efficient lighting solutions for ponds and water features. Intelligent lighting systems can create dynamic effects, and some are programmable to change based on the time of day or special events, enhancing the aesthetic appeal while conserving energy.

So many people, when you mention colour-changing lights, are put off because of their interpretation. If budget isn't an issue, I always recommend colour-changing lights because there are 12 different types of white light, believe it or not. Some clients initially opposed the idea of coloured lights. However, after installation, they often enjoy the different colour variations and may opt for something other than white.

Remote Monitoring

The use of sensors and internet-connected devices for remote monitoring of water level, temperature, and quality is rising. This technology offers pond owners peace of mind and the ability to address issues, even when away quickly. I want to say, but this technology is all good as long as it works. I have heard a lot of stories where these devices failed, and aquatic life suffered. I wouldn't say I like remote monitoring. I prefer the natural approach, keeping free-range fish instead of intensely farmed fish that are constantly monitored. There is a time and a place. I'm not against it; it's just not my preferred method.

Innovation

Innovation is not merely an option but necessary in differentiating your business in the competitive pond market. It involves:

Design Innovation

Embracing creative and unique design concepts that enhance aesthetic appeal and improve functionality and sustainability. Think beyond traditional ponds to incorporate features like ecosystem ponds, natural swimming ponds, vertical water gardens, interactive water features that engage the senses, or fountainscapes (a "fountainscape" is a decorative water feature that integrates a fountain or series of fountains into a landscape, typically focusing on the movement and sound of water through sculptural elements or spouts without necessarily incorporating aquatic life).

Material and Technological Advancements
Utilising the latest materials that offer durability and environmental benefits, and adopting cutting-edge pond management technology can significantly improve efficiency and appeal. For instance, intelligent monitoring systems, energy-efficient pumps, and advanced filtration techniques can give customers lower maintenance and higher satisfaction.

R&D Investment
Even small businesses can invest in research and development by experimenting with new ideas on a small scale, talking with academic institutions, or engaging with innovation hubs. Continuous improvement and willingness to try new approaches can lead to breakthroughs that differentiate your offerings.

Eric Triplett, also known as "The Pond Digger", invented The Helix™ Pond Skimmer, which won the "Product of the Year 2012" award in Pond Trade Magazine. The product is fish-friendly and removes debris efficiently, setting a new standard for filtration efficiency and fish safety. This propelled Eric's business to new heights and established his company as a leading provider of pond filtration solutions for dedicated koi ponds and other water gardens.

Emerging Opportunities

Therapeutic Water Features (healing gardens with water)
The growing recognition of the mental and physical health benefits of being close to water has led to therapeutic water features within healing gardens. These spaces promote relaxation, reduce stress, and offer a tranquil environment for contemplation and recovery. Incorporating elements like gentle standalone waterfalls, reflective pools, and softly bubbling streams, these features are becoming popular in hospitals, wellness centres, and private residences, seeking to harness water's therapeutic properties.

Cory Mann, the owner of Poseidon Ponds & Landscaping, exemplifies how integrating sustainability and innovation can lead to remarkable success stories. By creating a beautiful, therapeutic pond for Brett, who lost sight following lung transplant surgery, Mann showcased the profound impact of a pond beyond aesthetics. This project highlights the therapeutic potential of water features, emphasising sensory experiences like the sound of water, which can provide immense psychological benefits. The pond became a hobby for Brett and a source of therapy, illustrating the influential role of sustainable, thoughtfully designed water features in improving quality of life. This case underscores the importance of considering the user's needs and the environmental impact, illustrating that sustainability and innovation can create significant spaces.

Urban Ponds (*pond in a pot, patio ponds and bowls*)
With urbanisation limiting the availability of large outdoor spaces, there's an increasing trend towards creating small-scale water features that fit into compact urban settings. Patio pot ponds and water bowls offer a solution for city dwellers to enjoy the beauty and tranquillity of a pond without requiring a traditional garden space. These features can transform balconies, rooftops, and small patios into peaceful retreats, bringing a touch of nature to the urban environment and opening up the pond market to a broader audience. I like simple ornamental spitters and fountain heads, and I remember the giggling and gurgling rocks.

Integrated Aquaponic Systems (*you can have your pond and eat it*)
Aquaponics combines aquaculture (raising fish) with hydroponics (growing plants without soil) in a symbiotic environment. Integrated aquaponic systems are gaining traction as they offer a sustainable method of producing food whilst enjoying a pond's aesthetic and ecological

benefits. These systems allow homeowners to grow vegetables and herbs directly from their pond's nutrient-rich water, providing a source of fresh produce alongside the enjoyment of water gardening. This "edible" water feature concept appeals to the growing interest in self-sufficiency, organic gardening, and sustainable living practices. You don't even need high-tech systems. You can grow food on floating islands. One of my personal favourites is watercress. One thing to know about eating from your garden pond is you must be careful of what you're treating the pond with. If the fish becomes sick and you need to treat it, note that adding any chemicals into the pond means you'll also be eating them.

Sustainable Solutions and Climate Change
The increasing awareness of climate change and environmental degradation has spurred interest in sustainable landscape solutions, with ponds playing a crucial role. Ponds and water features are being recognised for their aesthetic value and ability to contribute positively to the environment. They can enhance local biodiversity, provide natural cooling in urban areas, and manage stormwater runoff, helping mitigate the impacts of heavy rainfall and reduce urban heat islands. Additionally, ponds can be integrated into rainwater harvesting systems, further aligning with sustainable practices by conserving water resources. This growing interest positions ponds as vital elements in eco-

friendly landscaping strategies that address climate change challenges, offering beauty and ecological benefits.

Making a Difference

Succeeding in the pond industry transcends technical prowess and business savvy; it's rooted in a commitment to sustainability, enriching the community, and embracing continuous learning. By fostering eco-friendly practices, engaging with local initiatives, and pursuing knowledge, pond professionals can make a meaningful difference, transforming landscapes and lives.

Understanding and leveraging industry trends is crucial to success in the pond industry. The alignment of innovative practices with sustainability principles sets businesses apart and ensures their long-term viability and positive impact on the environment.

In the pond industry, your work does more than transform outdoor spaces—it enriches lives, strengthens community bonds, and champions environmental conservation. Imagine creating serene havens where families gather, friends reconnect, and nature thrives. Each pond is a testament to your dedication to sustainability and a gift of tranquillity and beauty to the world. Let your passion inspire you to design water features that are not just visually stunning but also meaningful spaces where memories are made, fostering well-being and connecting people to the natural world.

Importance of Sustainability

Sustainability in the pond industry encompasses eco-friendly practices like using renewable resources and minimising pollution to protect the environment. Far from being just a trend, sustainability is essential for long-term business success and meeting customer expectations. Embracing these practices appeals to environmentally aware clients and meets regulatory standards, providing businesses with a competitive advantage.

Incorporating sustainable practices across all business operations, from design to maintenance, is crucial in the evolving pond industry. This shift highlights the growing emphasis on eco-friendly practices as a cornerstone of modern business strategies.

Eco-Friendly Practices
Ponds play a vital role in fostering sustainable ecosystems by supporting local wildlife and conserving water. Sustainable pond design and construction prioritise native plants, solar-powered equipment, and natural

filtration systems to create balanced, environmentally friendly water features.

Sustainability as a Business Strategy

Adopting eco-friendly practices sets your business apart and attracts environmentally-conscious consumers. This strategic focus on sustainability promotes business growth and benefits the environment over the long term.

For those in the pond industry looking to deepen their commitment to sustainability, numerous websites and online courses offer guidance on eco-friendly business practices, providing valuable resources for continuous learning and improvement.

Forging Your Path with Confidence

The pond industry presents a dynamic landscape of challenges and opportunities for new entrants and seasoned professionals. Embracing these with confidence and a strategic approach can lead to a successful business and a positive impact on communities and the environment.

For Newcomers: Building a Strong Foundation

Entering the pond industry is an exciting journey that requires a blend of creativity, technical skill, and ecological awareness.

Here's how to start:

- **Master the basics**

    Gain a solid understanding of design principles, construction techniques, and the ecological aspects of pond ecosystems. This foundational knowledge is crucial for creating sustainable and aesthetically pleasing water features.

- **Seek professional development**

    Enhance your skills and credibility through certifications, workshops, and joining industry associations. These resources offer valuable learning opportunities and networking platforms to connect with peers and experts.

For Experienced Professionals: Staying Ahead of the Curve

For those with established careers in the pond industry, continuous innovation and learning are crucial to maintaining competitiveness and growth.

- **Embrace technology**

    Stay updated with the latest pond technology, from intelligent monitoring systems to eco-friendly filtration. Leveraging these advancements can improve efficiency, sustainability and client satisfaction.

- **Expand your offerings**

    Consider broadening your services to include emerging trends like therapeutic water features or integrated aquaponic systems. Diversification can attract new clients and open up additional revenue streams.

- **Foster partnerships**

    Collaborating with landscapers, environmentalists, and suppliers can enhance your service quality and offer comprehensive solutions to clients.

- **Commit to learning**

    The pond industry is ever-evolving, with new research, environmental regulations, and consumer preferences shaping the market. Continuous education ensures you remain at the forefront, ready to adapt and innovate.

PART 2: CRAFTING YOUR UNIQUE OFFER

"Innovation distinguishes between a leader and a follower."
- Steve Jobs

3
DESIGNING WITH CREATIVITY

This chapter delves into the essence of aquatic art. This creative approach emphasises the seamless integration of design principles with the practicalities of pond construction, exploring the intricate layers of personal expression and the harmonious relationship between the designer, the water feature, and its environment.

Aquatic art is not merely about enhancing the visual appeal of gardens but about forging ecosystems that flourish in harmony with their natural surroundings. It is a testament to the belief that the true beauty of a water feature lies not only in its ability to captivate the senses but also in its contribution to the sustainability of the local environment.

Aquatic art's heart lies in a profound respect for the balance between aesthetics, functionality, and ecology. Water features are an art that goes beyond traditional design boundaries. By understanding the fundamentals of design and acknowledging the crucial role of natural elements—rock formations, aquatic plants, and fish—aquatic artists can craft water features that integrate flawlessly with the landscape and support and enrich the local ecosystem. The aim is to transcend traditional landscaping to create aquatic masterpieces that are serene, functional, and mindful of water conservation.

Fundamental Principles of Aquatic Art & Design

By exploring the fundamental principles below, you can embark on your design journeys, creating water features that are as functional as they are enchanting. This will ensure success and fulfilment in the pond business.

Balance and Proportion
It is crucial to ensure the water feature blends seamlessly with the surrounding landscape. This can be achieved by considering its location, shape, and placement in relation to the size of the garden, the house, and the scale of the feature itself. The designer's ability to balance, proportion, and integrate these elements into the garden

canvas can transform a simple pond into a living work of art.

Unity and Harmony

When designing a garden, the water feature must align with the theme and style. This can be achieved using materials, colours and plantings that harmonise with the overall design.

Movement and Sound

Incorporating elements that add movement, such as waterfalls, streams or fountains, can create a visually dynamic garden and also produce soothing sounds. The sound of running water can create a peaceful garden oasis that attracts wildlife. However, some people prefer a space that reflects natural elements without the sound of water. In such cases, we can use aeration to maintain the water quality or grow more water plants to achieve a natural still water effect.

Focal Point

A focal point is an essential element in a garden, as it creates a visual anchor that draws the eye and invites you to explore the space. A water feature can be a central gathering spot or a destination for contemplation, where you can interact with fish or other elements. Water has a powerful draw, similar to the allure of light from a fire, and it naturally attracts us towards it.

Symphony of Textures

Texture is critical in the tactile experience of a garden water feature. Simply changing the flow rate can change the texture of the water's surface, which in turn changes an onlooker's mood and emotions. A symphony of textures enhances the visual appeal and invites physical interaction, encouraging visitors to touch, feel, and connect with the elemental aspects of water.

Some examples include:
- The contrast between the smooth water surface and the rough natural stone on a calm summer evening.
- The softness of underwater aquatic plant foliage moving in the flow, in contrast to the spiky plants that existed during the time of dinosaurs.
- The sleekness of modern materials that can create a rich tapestry of sensations.

So many people are drawn to touch show-stopping water features that one gets a real buzz when people ask, "Is this real? It looks so natural". They can't believe it when you tell them it is less than a week old. People love the feeling you can create, and often, they need to check in with themselves.

Water Filtration Integration

Proper water filtration is essential for preserving the health and hygiene of a water feature. Effective filtration systems that blend with the aesthetics must be integrated to maintain the beauty of the water feature. Whether chemical or natural, it should not compromise the ecological balance of the surrounding area or water in the feature.

Naturalism and Mimicry

Aquatic artists often use natural materials, such as natural stones and wood (i.e. incorporating natural dead and driftwood), to create an aged water environment resembling mature watercourses. This can enhance the sense of tranquillity and immersion for many designs that aim to replicate natural water environments.

I love the instant impact a weathered oak stump creates, and then I get lost in all the moss and miniature plants around it. The choice of stone and wood can dictate the water feature's integration with the surrounding landscape. Natural materials ensure the feature complements the garden's existing elements, fostering a cohesive and organic look.

Ecological Integration

When designing a garden water feature, it's essential to consider the local ecosystem by incorporating native plants, providing habitats for wildlife and using eco-friendly construction methods. This helps ensure that the water feature contributes positively to the garden's biodiversity. Proper plant selection enhances the pond's aesthetic and ecological stability. Tailored plant packages can help clients maintain a visually appealing and healthy pond environment.

Lighting and Night Appeal

The play of light and shadow is an often overlooked aspect of water feature design. Carefully placing a pond or a stream can capture the dance of sunlight throughout the day (I especially love looking at rays of reflecting sunlight rippling up a rock or a nearby tree). Still, at night, you, the artist, bring that magic with strategic lighting, casting ethereal glows and shadows, transforming the water feature into a nocturnal spectacle. This interplay adds a layer of complexity and allure, making each design a unique experience bound by natural light cycles.

Incorporating lighting in and around a water feature can highlight its elements after dark, extending the enjoyment of the space into the evening and adding a dramatic effect. It's often overlooked that seasonal colours can be enhanced through lighting. I enjoy driving up my road at night to see my house illuminated with rippling movement from the underwater lights in my spillway bowls. Incorporating illumination packages transforms the pond from a daytime attraction to a night-time spectacle. Understanding how to integrate lighting effectively can dramatically enhance the pond's appeal and functionality, offering clients round-the-clock enjoyment.

The Rhythm of Seasons

Designing with the rhythm of the seasons in mind ensures that a water feature remains a focal point of beauty and interest throughout the year. Seasonal changes bring new dimensions to the garden, with flowering aquatic plants, autumnal reflections and even the stark beauty of a frost-kissed pond in winter. A designer skilled in the art of seasonal planning can create a water feature that is ever-evolving, celebrating the transient beauty of nature. You can enjoy these features 365 days a year by bringing them close to the house. Imagine having a watering hole right by your patio that you can see from your favourite chair.

Accessibility and Safety

Accessibility and safety are crucial to ensuring a water feature is easily accessible and safe for maintenance and enjoyment. This involves considering edge treatments, stepping stones, and viewing platforms. It is essential to ensure that friends and relatives who visit your customer's water feature have a positive experience. Some features may be safer than others, and it is essential to note that the water itself is not the problem but rather the feature's design. Early interactions with garden water features can provide tremendous benefits and teach valuable life skills.

Sustainability and Conservation

Water features can be created and maintained in an eco-friendly manner by utilising sustainable practices, such as rainwater harvesting and natural filtration systems. These methods can help to reduce any potential harm to the environment. Solar-powered pumps can be used for small garden water features. However, I have yet to come across any large standalone solar-powered pumps that can operate without big solar panels or large batteries powering our standard eco-friendly pumps. Designing ponds that support local wildlife, including features like bog pockets and beaches, adds value to any garden space. It enriches biodiversity and creates a more engaging and natural pond environment.

Customisation and Personalisation

Many individuals have an unacknowledged desire to have a water feature in their garden. Creating a water feature that caters to various preferences and lifestyles is possible. Water in the garden can serve a variety of purposes. This method ensures that the water feature satisfies the aesthetic and functional needs, whilst reflecting the homeowners' personality and values.

Decorative features like stacked slate walls and spheres add visual interest and depth. Employing design principles, such as the rule of thirds, ensures these elements are placed in a way that is visually balanced and engaging.

Effect of Feedback on Creativity and Style

Understanding what people like and dislike is vital. The best way I found that I had chosen the right style for myself was by building features at shows. You get to be the fly on the wall when many people are around your display garden. And as you stand, you hear the real unfiltered comments as you are almost in the conversations next to your aquatic art.

Here are two memories that will last a lifetime:

The first was early on at a local flower show. A lady stopped me as I was dead-heading and asked if she could remove her shoes. She wanted to connect with nature and thanked me before moving on. It's incredible what you created in such a small space.

The second was when I won runner-up Best in Show at Hampton Court in 2016, the biggest flower show in the world. I remember that on press day before, all the judges had been around a child (with his teacher) who wanted to talk to me after discovering that I had designed and built the feature. The gardening press and media were queuing with questions that day, and he wanted to get in line. The little man said, "If I were an ant, I would want to live there." At that moment, I felt like the Willy Wonka of Water Features. That child helped me think differently about our world (a world of pure imagination).

As you can see, it's so rewarding when you find your niche inspiring people of all ages. I feel a real sense of pride when I can assist my clients – even if it's the local wildlife. It took a long time to understand how powerful it was to inspire people to think differently about bringing water into their gardens.

Creating Signature Designs

Create a unique signature element that stands out in all your designs. It could be a particular water flow technique, a specific plant palette or a distinctive rock formation. Aquatic artists take pleasure in bending water and controlling its flow. You can often see them specialising in creating waterfalls that mimic a particular natural landmark or using a specific type of local stone in all their designs. It's beautiful to recognise an artist's work by their rock formations or when others identify your style. Keep exploring and experimenting with your designs until you find one element that speaks to you and sets your work apart.

Each pond design below uniquely incorporates water into people's gardens, catering to different desires and requirements. From the lush and biodiverse natural pond to the sleek and refined formal architectural feature, it is crucial to understand the fundamentals of garden pond design to confidently embark on the pond design of your choice and create the desired lifestyle for your customers.

Stillwater Wildlife Pond Design
Particularly suited to the British garden, the Stillwater Wildlife Pond emphasises creating a habitat for native flora and fauna without continuous water movement. This design forgoes pumps and filtration, relying on the natural processes of plant life to maintain water quality. It would help if you "became" the mechanical filters sometimes and covered the ponds in the autumn. Only offer these ponds if you provide maintenance. It's a wildlife sanctuary, inviting birds, beautiful aquatic insects like dragonflies that do not sting or bite, and amphibians to dwell within the garden. By designing with native plants and shallow margins, ponds support local biodiversity and offer a peaceful, reflective water feature that blends seamlessly into the natural landscape.

Formal Architectural Pond Design

An addition to consider is the traditional architectural pond design, which combines geometric shapes and symmetrical layouts and often incorporates modern materials like glass or metal. This style is perfect for urban or contemporary gardens where the emphasis is on structure and formality. With clean, crisp lines and often featuring sculptures or fountains, these ponds are designed as much for their visual impact as for the sound and movement of water they provide. Though they may require a lot more precise engineering, filtering, maintenance and chemicals, especially in water clarity and feature functioning, they do, however, add a dramatic and elegant touch to lots of spaces.

Ecosystem Ponds

The natural pond design mimics a wild pond's aesthetic and ecological balance, integrating rocks, gravel, and aquatic plants. This approach aims to create a self-sustaining ecosystem, where every element – from the microorganisms to the fish and plants – plays a crucial role in maintaining water quality and overall health. Ideal for those seeking to enhance their garden with a piece of nature, this design beautifies the landscape and serves as a haven for local wildlife, promoting biodiversity. Incorporating natural filtration methods through plant roots and gravel reduces the reliance on mechanical systems, making it a low-maintenance option for a tranquil retreat.

Dedicated Fish Pools

This fish-farming approach is geared towards koi carp (known as *nishikigoi*). The approach prioritises the health, growth, and visibility of fish above all. Suppose your enthusiastic customer wants to show their high-quality koi. In that case, this design is for them, as it's much easier to facilitate maintenance, like netting and inspecting the fish with a net and measuring bowl. This more traditional design uses bare surfaces (to avoid scale damage) and minimal plant life (think of a swimming pool with fish). These open systems (constant water changes) ensure gin clear water for enjoying fish viewing. These are often heated, and the growth rates are phenomenal due to all the new water.

These ponds are supported by the latest advanced innovations in pond filtration technology and aeration to keep the water pristine. Water quality management is needed to ensure the thriving of the fish; we tend to keep lots of fish in these systems, so naturally, it's more work. This type of filtration demands more attention (you can't get away with cleaning it once a year) and a more hands-on approach when you get an error code (as the solid waste has to be removed quickly). This pool design may also have potential limitations on the fish's natural behaviours due to the need for environmental features like substrate, rocks, and plants, which are found in more naturalistic ponds. Significantly, you will have a more challenging time making these pools look natural if the pool is raised due to the need for jump guards.

Free Range Koi Ponds
These ponds are pretty spacious, with the constructed wetland filtration and marginal areas taking up significant space. Keeping koi fish in these systems is akin to raising free-range chickens, cleaning the living space as needed (maybe once a year), and ensuring the water quality is conducive to a diverse ecosystem whilst providing clear areas to observe the fish's natural behaviour. By combining natural elements from high-flow river systems with fish farming principles, pond owners can enjoy both natural aquatic life areas and optimised fish health in a hybrid design.

This innovative approach divides the pond into zones dedicated to natural aquatic life areas for water plant growth and security, sometimes located next to the pond in a constructed wetland filter and areas optimised for fish health. I like to educate my clients that these systems are similar to coral reefs, with drop-off zones for the koi, referred to as freshwater cows or sharks by some people, as they eat lots of aquatic life and plants. It's great to watch the koi, like miniature freshwater killer whales, when hunting for natural food or pellets just out of reach. Thoughtful plant selection reduces the need for water chemistry management, which is essential to maintaining this delicate balance, offering a dynamic and interactive garden feature.

The field of aquatic design is a place where the beauty of nature meets human creativity, offering limitless possibilities for designers to express their unique vision. The essence of creative pond design is not limited to assembling elements but lies in viewing a garden as a canvas of infinite possibilities. It is an invitation to embark on a personal journey of discovery, where each water feature reflects the designer's unique perspective on beauty, nature, and sustainability. This journey encourages aquatic artists to push the boundaries of traditional design, exploring new materials, techniques, and ecological principles to create spaces that are not only visually stunning but also in harmony with the natural world.

Finding Your Niche in Garden Water Feature Design

Collecting ideas and inspirations (through an inspiration journal or a digital mood board) helps crystallise your dream pond design, guides your planning process, and ensures the result aligns with your vision.

Step One: Start with Imitation

When looking for inspiration, search the internet. Much like professional photographers (or someone learning to play the guitar) who want to specialise or pick up a new skill, they look at other photographers' work and try to copy the images (or they try to play other people's tunes first before finding the music). Garden Water Feature Designers and aquatic artists may find their niche by initially mimicking the work of others. This stage is crucial for mastering the foundational aspects of design. However, the goal should always be to evolve beyond someone else's imitation. Once you've honed your skills, begin experimenting with adapting elements to suit your emerging style. Again, expanding on photography as an analogy, consider photographers specialising in portrait or landscape photography. Each requires a unique set of skills, an understanding of composition, and a way of seeing the world. Similarly, as you develop your design style, consider whether you're more drawn to the "portrait" aspect (focusing on detailed, possibly manufactured decorative water features) or the "landscape" aspect (creating expansive, naturalistic designs with natural stone and wood). This focus will help you master your chosen domain.

Step Two: Reflect on Your Preferences

Analyse what draws you to specific designs. Is it the tranquillity of natural, meandering streams or the architectural precision of formal water features? Your preferences are the first indicator of your potential niche.

Step Three: Leverage Your Strengths

Assess your strengths. Are you skilled in creating habitats that support wildlife, or do you excel in integrating modern technology into your designs? Identifying and playing to your strengths can help you develop a signature style. Your unique experiences can also shape your design approach. Whether it's travel, hobbies, or a background in another field of design, these experiences can infuse your work with originality.

Step Four: Embrace Authenticity

Authenticity is magnetic. When your work genuinely reflects your values and aesthetics, it resonates with clients with similar tastes. This authentic connection sets your designs apart and builds a loyal client base.

Developing a unique design style is a journey of exploration and refinement. By reflecting on your preferences, leveraging your strengths, drawing from your experiences, and embracing authenticity, you can establish a distinctive presence in the garden water feature design industry. Remember, the most memorable and impactful designs often come from a place of genuine passion and personal connection to the work.

4

BUILDING WITH EXCELLENCE

Constructing ponds and garden water features for people is not just about digging a hole and filling it with water. It's a meticulous blend of art and science that involves careful planning. A business aims to be healthy, so I recommend that new business owners or budding artists use the available water feature kits to save time.

You can find fountain kits, standalone waterfall or stream kits, and several different pond kits (garden, pond kits with waterfalls, wildlife ponds, ecosystem pond kits) with everything you need. This way, you won't have to spend hours planning each time you want to build a water feature. However, adapting these kits to fit your unique creative vision within the given footprint guidelines is essential.

Every feature is still exceptional, as what you do with the kit is up to you; the rocks (or ways you use them) and surroundings are different. This chapter aims to guide you through the intricacies of pond construction and maintenance, enabling you to create a breathtaking water feature that is also environmentally friendly. The goal is to equip you with the knowledge and skills to build ponds and water features that can keep you trading and last a long time while enabling you to create aquatic art masterpieces.

Expanding construction basics in creating aquatic art, the journey from vision to reality is paved with several critical decisions, each shaping the path of the project and the life of the business. At the heart of building with excellence lies an understanding of construction basics, which allows artists and builders to create ponds and water features that reflect their passion and professionalism.

Foundations of Water Feature Construction

Thriving as a Solopreneur or Team Leader

The business model you adopt in aquatic design is not just a choice; it's a fundamental decision that shapes your entire construction approach. Whether you're a solo artisan crafting each project with your hands and heart or a visionary leading a team to execute grand designs, your business model defines how you operate. It's a choice between being intimately involved in every detail or stepping back to manage and direct. This decision impacts the scope of projects you undertake and the trajectory of your business and personal life.

As you develop in business, your role might change. It is essential to keep in mind and prepare for the future. Our bodies tend to slow down as we age, and we must adjust accordingly. To maximise your earnings, you should focus on managing others. On the other hand, if you prefer complete control, you should pick the projects you can handle and excel at on your own. You can build fantastic water features without huge rocks or machinery; these are more like garden water features, but you can still create aquatic art.

Artistry vs. Traditional Construction
The distinction between an aquatic artist and a traditional pond builder is not just a matter of technique; it's a profound difference in approach. An artist's canvas curves with the landscape, never confined by straight lines or conventional boundaries. Suppose you enjoy thinking innovatively. Are you constantly seeking to redefine the concept of a box? This creative freedom often commands a higher value, allowing you to charge for the

construction, vision, and uniqueness you bring. It's a testament to the belief that what you create isn't just a water feature — it's a piece of living art.

Designing with Purpose and Passion

The essence of your work lies in answering the simple yet profound question, "I'm happy when?" Only a few business owners ask themselves this question, which is pivotal to identifying what makes them the happiest, whether the scale of the projects, the type of clients, or the style of features that brings them joy. This knowledge shapes every decision, from project selection to the design process, aligning your business with your fulfilment.

Balancing Passion with Practicality

Every builder dreams of delivering perfection, but budgets and timelines govern the reality of construction. The art of construction is not just in the creation but in aligning vision with practical constraints. Ensuring that the project's scale, complexity, and costs are in harmony is not just a challenge; it's necessary for both client satisfaction and business viability. Tracking the time you take to build a project allows you to understand your numbers when faced with the same project the next time it crops up or if you need to adjust pricing structures.

Physical and Business Sustainability

The physical demands of water feature construction are undeniable. Recognising your limits and planning for longevity means considering how many projects you can realistically handle before wear and tear take their toll. Similarly, project selection — choosing which ventures to undertake — can define your brand and influence growth. Deciding to stay lean with much lower overheads or expand with a team is associated with picking the size of a 'business backpack' you're prepared to carry.

Do you want to focus on a niche within the market with a highly specialised solution, which in turn commands a king's ransom? Or do you want to build a water feature brand to have a broader impact? The best way is to expand by building a team, opening new locations, and investing in marketing campaigns.

Site Analysis and Design Consultation

This initial paid phase is critical in protecting both you and your client. A thorough site analysis and an open, honest design consultation set the stage for a successful project. It's about creating a water feature that meets the client's desires and expectations while being feasible and sustainable within the landscape. This stage is not just about envisioning the garden water feature but ensuring its viability, longevity, and the satisfaction of all involved.

Charging for the site analysis and design consultation can be a valuable investment, demonstrating your expertise and commitment. This fee can be carried forward and deducted from the project cost if the salesperson successfully closes the project, ensuring the client sees value in your initial efforts.

Technical Skills Needed

Exploring the technical aspects of pond construction and water feature installation is not just about following steps; it's about understanding the synergy between the landscape, the water, and the life it supports. This deep dive into technical skills goes beyond the basics to explore the nuances that elevate a project from functional to exceptional. The satisfaction of obtaining these skills is not just a professional achievement but a personal one that can fuel your passion and drive for excellence.

Excavation

The first cut into the earth is where the vision takes shape. But excavation is more than just digging a hole; it's about sculpting the land to welcome water. Understanding soil types, slope stability, and drainage patterns is crucial. Excavating with the foresight of how water moves through the landscape can prevent future issues such as erosion or sedimentation. This understanding enhances your technical skills and connects you to the environment, making you a responsible steward of the land.

Liner Installation

A pond's liner is its skin (the waterproof bag if you like), holding the lifeblood of water within. The choice between flexible liners, pre-formed shells, or concrete constructions depends on the design and purpose of the water features. Proper installation is paramount to avoid water loss, leaks or low edges, exposed unprotected liners with wrinkles, and common settling.

Tips include:
- Ensuring the use of over and underlay as needed.
- Installing the correct amount of freeboard (the space between the top of the water and the overflow point).
- Protecting against sharp objects in and around the pond.
- At times, material expansion and contraction become necessary due to changes in temperature or weather conditions.

Seaming Liners

For more significant water features or ones that need extending where a single liner won't suffice, mastering the art of seaming liners together to ensure a watertight finish is crucial. This skill requires precision and understanding of the materials to prevent leaks.

Strapping Rocks

In bigger or more complicated installations, machinery or teams of people are necessary to strategically place and secure large rocks and boulders for the water feature. This process requires knowledge of strapping, lifting techniques, machinery operation, and safety protocols to ensure the structural integrity of the water feature and the safety of all involved.

Detailed Edge Treatments

The pond's edge is where the water meets the land, and mastery in creating natural, seamless transitions can significantly enhance the feature's aesthetic. Techniques may include strategically placing stones, plants, and other materials to hide liners and create a more natural appearance.

Bending Water

This is an advanced skill that involves manipulating water flow to achieve specific visual and auditory effects, such as creating meandering streams or dramatic waterfalls. It involves echo chambers, pinch points, switchbacks, and combination falls. This requires a deep understanding of rock placement, pump capacities, sealing voids, and the contours you create.

Recreating Nature

Beyond basic construction, the ability to mimic natural processes and aesthetics in a controlled pond environment demands a keen eye for detail and a broad knowledge of natural ecosystems. Recreating nature involves selecting the right mix of flora and fauna, understanding natural water cycles, and replicating natural landforms.

Mixing Elements

Just as an artist uses a palette of colours, aquatic artists use a mix of elements (water, stone, drift and dead wood, plant life and foliage, and lighting) to create a cohesive and captivating design. The best way to learn is to play, so experiment with diverse materials and textures in your gardens or friends' gardens. This is how you can develop and inspire others with creativity and uniqueness in your projects.

Working Within Constraints

Whether it's a limited budget, space, or specific client requirements, the ability to adapt and innovate within constraints is a valuable skill.

Constraints might involve:

- Selecting cost-effective materials.
- Designing for smaller spaces.

- Finding creative solutions to meet clients' desires without compromising quality or aesthetics.

Filtration System Setups

As mentioned before, not all water features need filtration. However, they all do need management. The heart of a healthy garden pond lies in its filtration system, pumping life by cleaning and oxygenating the water. Different pond styles (from natural earth in stillwater wildlife ponds to sophisticated koi habitats) demand tailored filtration solutions. Exploring the balance between mechanical, biological, and chemical filtration techniques is critical.

Water Quality Management

Clear, healthy water is the lifeblood of any pond or water feature. Mastery here involves regular monitoring and adjustments to parameters such as pH, ammonia, nitrites, and oxygen levels. Educate yourself on the ecosystems you're creating; knowing how to diagnose and rectify water quality issues quickly will ensure the vitality of the pond's inhabitants and the longevity of the feature. Your role in maintaining this delicate balance is crucial, as it directly impacts the health and well-being of the aquatic life you've nurtured.

Continuous Learning

The field of aquatic landscaping is ever-evolving, with new materials, technologies, and ecological insights constantly emerging. Staying abreast of these developments requires a commitment to education. Learning might mean attending workshops, enrolling in online courses, or participating in industry conferences.

Hands-on experience, paired with this ongoing professional development, solidifies your technical skills and keeps you at the forefront of the field. Working with others in the industry will help form bonds and a trusted network to call upon when needed. You can be a contractor for hire on a day rate plus expenses. Joining forces as needed and hiring people above your skill set might not be cost-effective for that single project, but the golden nuggets will pay you back in the long term.

In marrying technical proficiency with an artist's touch, you construct water features and create ecosystems and sanctuaries of beauty. This holistic understanding and skill set ensures that each project meets the client's and landscape's immediate needs and contributes positively to the local environment, securing your legacy of aquatic artistry.

Creative Design Solutions

Success often hinges on navigating challenges with innovative and creative design solutions. These solutions solve practical problems and elevate garden water feature aesthetics and ecological values.

Integrating Naturalistic Features

The essence of creating a naturalistic water feature lies in its seamless blend with the surrounding landscape, mimicking the beauty and complexity of nature. One innovative approach uses the existing topography to dictate the pond's location, shape and flow, incorporating locally found rocks, plants, and even soil types to enhance its natural appearance.

To give you an example of integrating naturalistic features, after working on maintaining a large garden pond, I was employed and commissioned to design and build a show-stopping water feature for a retiring couple who wanted to keep a main garden pond with the island but had water issues on the lawn. They wanted more water like their second home in France, which had a natural stream.

To set the scene, it's a vast garden in the Midlands, England, where there was a natural slope away from the house looking over to farmland. Usually, I would recommend getting the feature to a patio or destination spot, but this one called for working with what was in front of me. So we transformed a sloped garden with three water features that all looked like one huge feature. At the top, by the patio, we had a 12-metre-long standalone garden stream that looked like it had disappeared under the patio and come back up again at another point, flowing down a cascading stream that fed into the main pond.

To add more interest we didn't stop there — we also built the third feature off the back of this main pond to make it look like the pond was overflowing with joy into another standalone waterfall/stream. A large basin solved the water drainage issue and created a stunning focal point while attracting local wildlife. Creating a lovely walk around the whole garden, with benches at each destination point, I incorporated stepping stones over two of the three streams and cut a path through a wildflower meadow if they wanted to ride instead of walk.

Creating Wildlife Habitats

More clients are seeking ponds that support local ecosystems. Creative solutions here involve designing ponds with varied depth zones to cater to different species, from shallow areas for amphibians to deeper zones for fish. Incorporating submerged and marginal plant zones adds to the pond's beauty and provides essential habitats and breeding grounds. A case study worth noting is a pond we designed and built after a consumer called us when she was scared to put the frog-killing pump on.

In this pond, frogs, newts and toads were being killed daily by a considerable-sided fountain pump with a stainless steel cage that would suck up and trap them against the pre-filter. We changed the design and installed a wildlife-friendly intake bay where aquatic life can crawl and mate in the shallow water happily, and this stopped the aggressive pump sitting at the bottom of the system which was killing the reason she wanted the pond in the first place. The water was then delivered to an up-flow wetland filter, creating a natural cleaning system while offering another place for the amphibians to be happy. Not only that, but this was a habitat for a wide range of insects and birds, thus enhancing local biodiversity and promoting environmental responsibility.

Implementing Rainwater Harvesting Systems

Combining pond construction with rainwater harvesting is an innovative solution that addresses water conservation challenges. Designing ponds to double as rainwater collection areas provides a sustainable water source for the pond and can also alleviate drainage issues in the surrounding landscape.

However, you don't always need a pond to collect rainwater. We have one at POND College that collects the water off a barn roof. This one has a sustainable water feature that keeps the water fresh and clean, waters the gardens, and tops up all the ponds on site. I am amazed that so many farm buildings don't collect rainwater for their fields, let alone homeowners with vegetable gardens; no hose pipe bans here. You can install these systems with a downspout filtration, which reduces the property's overall water footprint.

Working in Small Spaces
Another creative project involved transforming a small urban garden into a thriving wildlife pond with a self-sustaining ecosystem. Despite space constraints, the pond design included a vertical garden wall that doubled as a biofilter. Bees loved this dripping biological water wall, which maximises the area's ecological and aesthetic value. The pond water stays crystal clear all the time due to the size of the feature. This project exemplifies how innovative thinking can overcome spatial limitations to create a vibrant, wildlife-friendly water feature in an urban setting, a true testament to the beauty and functionality of creative pond designs.

Overcoming Construction Challenges

Pond construction often faces challenges like unstable soil, which requires reinforcement techniques, and managing water flow to prevent erosion. Solutions include using geotextile for soil stability and designing overflow systems for effective water management. Drawing on expert advice ensures the structural integrity and longevity of the pond. Specialising in areas like koi ponds or natural swimming pools can set you apart. Specialisation demonstrates your commitment to excellence and can open new opportunities in the pond construction industry.

Don't forget to document projects with photos, videos, and website case studies. It showcases your work's quality and diversity, helping attract clients and build your brand. Use social media and a professional website to share your portfolio, highlighting your unique approach and successful projects.

Excellence in pond construction is achieved through technical skill, innovation, and creativity. By committing to continuous learning and applying innovative solutions to challenges, you can create ponds that are not only aesthetically pleasing but also ecologically sustainable, leaving a lasting impact on landscapes and communities.

5

MAINTENANCE MASTERY

A proactive maintenance approach can uncover opportunities for upgrades and enhancements, deepening the client relationship. Regular check-ins become moments to discuss new technologies, design trends, or expansions, positioning yourself as the pond professional as a trusted advisor rather than just a service provider. Maintenance can build trust, repeat business, and a reputation for excellence. Implementing a structured system for managing expectations and establishing transparent processes became crucial.

Starting my pond business from the ground up, maintenance wasn't just a strategy but a revelation. The breakthrough was supporting a local aquatic shop that wanted the staff to focus on their jobs, something other than moonlighting.

During these early days, I was often knee-deep in the water of various systems, always covered in pond juice. I began to see the divide between what worked and what faltered. Maintenance wasn't just about upkeep; it was my window into the soul of pond design and customer satisfaction. Yet, as the number of customers expanded, the challenge wasn't just the systems themselves but aligning subcontractors with the high standards of service I envisioned—where excellence wasn't an aspiration but a given. My standard is five stars, rising to even seven as needed, which is hard to transfer to a team.

The path to innovation, my quest for delivering unparalleled service and being rewarded for my efforts, led me to travel across the big pond to America to create low-maintenance water features and make more money. The goal was to transcend beyond repairing traditional bare liner features to crafting freshwater rock pools. These water features stood out as ideals of beauty and functionality, freeing me from endless fixes and ugly bodies of water. I was a pond guy who happened to run a business, and the support I found in America helped me transform into a business guy who still works with ponds and other garden water features.

Structuring success and adopting a premium but fair service call fee transformed how I approached maintenance, giving me the time and respect needed.

I weeded out the time wasters and people who expected something for nothing. This wasn't about charging more; it was about valuing my expertise and ensuring I could deliver that extra mile of service without diluting my worth. By refining my approach to maintenance, I inadvertently opened doors to deeper relationships, upgrades, and upselling opportunities.

This wasn't just about making jobs easier; it was about elevating the entire experience for everyone involved, from my team to our clients and their gardeners. Custom maintenance plans are pivotal. They reflect a deep understanding of each unique ecosystem and clients' preferences, ensuring that the service resonates with their expectations and fosters lasting relationships.

Managing diverse customer expectations is crucial to pond maintenance, as clients' preferences vary widely. Some clients are hands-on enthusiasts who enjoy tinkering with their systems, while others prefer a hands-free approach. Successful pond maintenance requires a balance between providing knowledge and resources to empower hands-on clients and creating unobtrusive maintenance plans for hands-free clients. Regular consultations and check-ins are essential for adjusting maintenance plans as clients' interests evolve. Ultimately, the goal is to foster relationships built on trust, respect, and mutual understanding, ensuring every water feature is a source of joy and satisfaction for your clients.

A reliable maintenance company always starts by proactively seeking maintenance contracts. This proactive approach is about growing the business and building trust, addressing small yet significant concerns that can lead to more substantial projects, and establishing a foundation for a successful enterprise. The critical ingredient for a successful maintenance service is transparent and consistent communication. Educating clients about the intrinsic value of regular upkeep reinforces the importance of their investment and establishes a foundation of trust and reliability.

From maintenance to major projects, a seemingly routine service call blossomed into a 114k project, unravelling a domino effect of opportunities that amounted to 500k across multiple properties. This wasn't luck; it resulted from a steadfast commitment to maintenance and the relationships it built. It underscored a powerful lesson: maintenance isn't just the backbone of a thriving pond business—it's the springboard for growth, innovation, and, ultimately, a legacy.

Key Focus Areas for Maintenance

Here are some of the most pressing needs of pond and water feature owners. Our recommendation is to establish a viable but indispensable water feature business. Highlighting these services in your offerings will demonstrate your comprehensive understanding of maintenance and commitment to ensuring the health and beauty of your clients' water features. This approach not only solves immediate problems for your garden water feature owners but also builds a foundation for a trusted and sought-after business that prioritises the longevity and satisfaction of its customers.

Custom Maintenance Plans

Develop tailored maintenance plans for each water feature, considering its size, design complexity, and the owner's lifestyle. Offering flexible maintenance schedules can accommodate owners who prefer minimal involvement and those who enjoy hands-on care. These plans, ranging from essential to all-encompassing AAA packages, should cater to varying needs, guaranteeing the water's health across seasons and over the years. As you can tell, I have been doing this for years and recommend you start with the essentials package, then include others as you see fit, for example, Silver (if needed), Gold, and Platinum. Please note we do not offer Bronze or basic packages. We found customers didn't like the names (same service, different names).

Algae Management

Understanding and implementing effective strategies for algae control is crucial. Offering services like regular cleanings, installation of UV clarifiers (chemical filtration is sometimes needed with bare-liner ponds and pools), and advising on nutrient management can become a significant part of your business (regular income each spring).

Aesthetic Enhancements

We offer services that enhance the visual appeal of water features, such as seasonal plantings, lighting upgrades, and decorative elements. This caters to owners who want to refresh or improve their water feature's aesthetics regularly.

Water Clarity Solutions

Develop expertise in maintaining crystal clear water through proper filtration systems, natural clarifiers, and balanced fish-feeding practices. Providing regular maintenance services to manage these factors can set your business apart.

Equipment Maintenance and Repair

Offering routine checks and maintenance for pumps, filters, and other equipment can prevent failures. Building a reputation for reliable equipment upkeep will attract and retain customers. Simplify the number of products (only carry a few different pump sizes) to have stock in your vehicle. At first, I would change a pump for the same size, but then I adopted 5 sizes only; you can fit most garden water features into these 5 offerings, and custom features can also be managed but at a premium rate.

Fish Health Monitoring

If trained, offer health check services for pond fish, including water testing and mucus scrapes. Make water-based treatment recommendations; however, do not go further than this. Express that you are not a vet. "Bring in the professionals, as needed" (https://www.fishvetsociety.org.uk/find-a-vet/).

As a fish GP, you can address one of the pond owners' main concerns: ensuring their aquatic pets thrive. Just don't pretend to be a specialist if you are not. Customers will soon turn sour if you advise them wrongly. Be honest; they will stand by your side, giving you better reviews and talking about you with their friends.

Invasive Plant Control

Providing services for controlling and removing invasive plants and advising on plant selection that enhances biodiversity without overtaking the pond can be a unique selling point. We have many earth-in-farm ponds in Northamptonshire that need reed control. You can offer this service and earn great money for hard work. If you need to gain dry suit experience, then get some training. We only provide water work, not moving waste. However, we give the customers support and education around it as it is more cost-effective for others to move the waste; you don't need skilled aquatic consultants to move the waste from the pond side away to waste after a few days. We do load trailers but don't move them as we have created a mess in the past, not knowing the grounds where the local ground maintenance team or the homeowners see the property much better.

Water Level Management

We offer leak detection services where we come out for three visits or offer a done-with-you service, supporting the client remotely. However, we constantly guard against not finding the cause of the water loss, as it's like finding a needle in a haystack without knowing the size or number of needles. As part of your maintenance service, you can install auto-fill systems and overflow to drainage.

Winterisation Services

We offer winter preparation services but keep most ponds open and running in the UK. Most water features are okay to be left running all year long, but you can also provide a service to cover these and stop the damage from the snow and ice. You can move pumps and change the systems around for the colder months. Some people want little pond heaters installed and advice on keeping a section of the pond unfrozen for gas exchange. This caters to your clients' seasonal needs.

Health and Safety Service Calls

Include services that ensure the water feature is safe and healthy, such as checking for electrical safety, water quality testing for features with wildlife, and providing structural integrity to prevent accidents.

Drainage and Filtration Maintenance

Specialising in regularly cleaning pumps, filters, skimmers, and drains to prevent blockages ensures the pond's filtration system runs efficiently, a critical service that pond owners need. Don't open or service filters you don't recommend, and install them due to small parts or opening up cans of worms. Having to return and fix the problems you created is a nightmare for everyone.

Aesthetic Enhancements

Offer services that enhance the visual appeal of water features, such as seasonal plantings, lighting upgrades, night-time illumination packages, and decorative elements. This caters to owners who want to refresh or enhance their water feature's aesthetics regularly.

Sound and Movement Adjustments

Tweaking or upgrading water features to alter or enhance water's sound and visual movement, meeting each owner's specific sensory preferences.

Automated Systems

Installing and maintaining automatic dosing systems for water treatment, photocell smart-colour-changing lights, and even auto feeders for growing on fish in garden ponds. These systems appeal to owners who desire the beauty and tranquillity of a water feature without the daily hands-on maintenance.

Emergency Services

Offering prompt emergency fish rehousing or moving services when people are suffering from water loss, pump failures, or other urgent issues are being addressed ensures water feature owners know who to call when problems arise, establishing your business as a reliable support system.

Educational Workshops

Conduct workshops or provide informational resources on water feature care, including DIY maintenance tips, seasonal care, and troubleshooting common problems. This helps build a community of informed owners and positions your business as an industry authority. Gardening clubs love speakers about mini water features, garden parties, or guided or self-guided tours.

Eco-Friendly Solutions

Provide expertise in eco-friendly options like rainwater harvesting systems integrated into water features, solar-powered pumps, and natural algae control methods. This attracts environmentally conscious owners.

Simplifying Water Feature Maintenance

The belief that garden water features require extensive work is a misconception often from poorly designed systems. Just as a disappointing meal at a restaurant reflects more on the chef than the ingredients, the functionality and upkeep of a water feature squarely rests on the designer's shoulders. "Don't blame the pond, blame the pond designer".

A well-conceived design should anticipate and address potential issues, ensuring the feature remains a source of pleasure, not a chore.

Encountering a high-maintenance DIY system left by previous homeowners poses unique challenges. While some enthusiasts relish their DIY filter systems, many prefer to enjoy their water feature's tranquillity without the hassle of constant upkeep and solving problems. I liken this to some people (primarily engineers) who like visiting a city's waste facility to see how it manages all the waste instead of enjoying what it offers. A problem in a DIY system for the designer or engineer is a quick fix; however, addressing these inherited systems requires patience and expertise, often necessitating hourly charges due to the complexity and unpredictability of the task at hand. Most people want it to be easy, so it's your job to help them.

Opting for a pond equipped with natural wetland filtration exemplifies a low-maintenance approach. Such systems, acting as biological filters, significantly reduce the necessity for chemical treatments, making maintenance less intensive than traditional garden upkeep. While the initial setup may require attention, wetland filters' longevity and simplicity and the pumps' strategic use provide a hassle-free experience, aligning with the desire for minimal intervention.

For those drawn to the beauty and serenity of koi ponds, understanding the importance of water quality management is paramount. Like managing waste in our homes, maintaining a healthy environment for koi is critical, with automated systems like drum filters aiding in this process. However, reliance on such technology demands vigilance and a readiness to address issues swiftly, underscoring the need for a thoughtful approach to design and maintenance.

Embracing Nature in Design for Ease and Efficiency

One pivotal lesson from my journey is the stark contrast in resilience between ecosystem ponds and traditional setups during power outages. Ecosystem ponds, designed in harmony with nature, demonstrate remarkable stability even in adversity, unlike their conventional counterparts, which can quickly become stressful with even short power cuts.

This understanding has steered me towards advocating for ecosystem-based designs whenever possible. By aligning with nature rather than attempting to control it, we set the stage for more forgiving systems that enrich the lives of both the inhabitants and the owners. In essence, the choice of the system—be it a self-regulating ecosystem or a meticulously managed koi pond—should reflect a balance between personal preference, ease of maintenance, and the inherent beauty and vitality of aquatic life.

By prioritising designs that complement nature's mechanisms, we can drastically reduce the labour and anxiety associated with pond maintenance, allowing owners to relish their water features' beauty. Whether it's through the strategic use of skimmers to prevent disaster or choosing filtration systems that align with a pond's natural ecology, our goal should always be to create spaces that thrive with minimal human intervention, thereby ensuring the longevity and enjoyment of these aquatic treasures.

The importance of designing water features with maintenance in mind must be considered. Clients who desire spectacular ponds with all the bells and whistles often overlook long-term maintenance implications. This can lead to algae blooms, clogged systems, and poor water quality, ultimately resulting in frustrated clients seeking the help of pond maintenance specialists. It is essential to approach each construction project with a maintenance-first mindset, ensuring the beauty created is sustainable, manageable, and enduring.

Education sessions with clients can help them understand the maintenance processes and tools required to keep their ponds in good condition. Working with Mother Nature, keeping the system simple, and having multiple pumps can help prevent significant problems and provide more time before maintenance issues arise. Proper pond skimmers can also be installed to prevent pet fish from dying due to lack of water in the event of plumbing issues.

Every year, we receive calls and messages from garden owners with large ponds that have become a problem. Inspired by the beautiful water features at garden shows, these owners have contacted garden designers or landscape gardeners to create an elaborate pond or water feature. The designer, driven by enthusiasm to make something with all the trimmings—a waterfall, a few koi carp, and water lilies—is focused on aesthetics and immediate gratification, with little regard for the long-term maintenance implications. This oversight is not due to negligence but rather a naive assumption that beauty and functionality are self-sustaining.

However, as time passes post-installation, the once idyllic water features start to reveal their hidden complexities. Algae blooms, exacerbated by inadequate filtration and excessive sunlight, turn the water from crystal clear to murky green. The waterfall, though stunning, becomes a conduit for debris, clogging the system and reducing water flow to a mere trickle. Once vibrant and active, the koi show signs of stress and poor health due to fluctuating water quality.

Frustrated and overwhelmed, the clients contact us as pond maintenance specialists for help. It's a complicated conversation as it's a wake-up call, sometimes the stark realisation that the designer and landscapers had inadvertently set the stage for future challenges in their pursuit of immediate beauty. The projects, intended to be impressive showcases, become a cautionary tale of what happens when maintenance is an afterthought. Often, there is no way to clean the system. When we talk to the designer or the landscapers, it's a mixed bag; some see it as good business (they have been paid, and now we are getting paid for our work; however, we prefer happy pond owners). In contrast, others say they are never building or designing water features again.

Education sessions with clients, designers and landscapers have become a priority. We want to ensure that they have the knowledge and tools to maintain the health and aesthetics of their pond. Some clients have taken our advice and upgraded to better wetland filtration systems. However, a major overhaul of filtration systems to address significant algae issues is only sometimes possible.

In such cases, we have to make do with adding products to contain the problems. More aquatic plantings can be introduced to provide natural shade and help remove nutrients.

Our principle is that maintenance should never be a secondary consideration. It should be a foundational aspect of the design process. Every construction project should be approached with a maintenance-first mindset. This ensures that the beauty we create is sustainable, manageable, and enduring.

"Content is king, but context is god."
- Gary Vaynerchuk

PART 3: GROWING YOUR BUSINESS

"People can be your greatest frustration and source of inspiration."

6

A GUIDE TO BUILDING YOUR BRAND

Branding goes beyond visual identifiers like logos and colour schemes. It is an art that tells your story about your water feature business in a way that resonates with your audience. Your brand reflects your creativity, commitment to excellence, and unique approach to harmonising natural beauty with functional design. It's about establishing a connection with potential clients that speaks not just to their eyes but also to their souls.

Effective branding involves carefully integrating your personal preferences, design style or tastes into a broader brand identity. This integration transforms your work from projects into stories, each with its identity, philosophy, and purpose. These stories become the pillars of your brand, distinguishing you in a crowded market and making your business seen and felt. You need something for people to lock onto, like your personality or beliefs. As Aquatic Artisans, we all do the same: Create a hole and fill it with water, so you need to find and add your flair.

Your portfolio serves as a canvas, showcasing your capabilities and the depth of your vision. Through storytelling, you invite potential clients into your world, offering them a glimpse of what lies beyond the water's surface. This narrative approach helps forge a deeper connection, turning casual viewers into committed clients. You don't need a considerable portfolio or to take on more significant projects to boost your profile. Once you decide what type of business you want, stick to your lane and focus all your efforts there. Don't showcase farm ponds or commercial work if you want to do more garden water features. You get what you sow.

The journey of branding is constant. Brands are ever-evolving, like the nature of water itself. It demands an ongoing commitment to innovation, adapting to the changing tides of market trends, and continuously exploring new ways to captivate and engage your audience. In this dynamic dance of creativity and commerce, your brand becomes a beacon, guiding clients to your doorstep, eager to experience the magic you create.

Understanding and implementing effective branding is not just about making your business known; it's about making it understood, appreciated and sought after. Consistency in your branding efforts, from your logo to your online presence, establishes a sense of reliability and trustworthiness. It's about creating a legacy that flows as freely and beautifully as the water features you design.

Developing a Visual Personal Brand

Crafting a personal brand that visually and emotionally resonates with your target market is crucial to distinguishing yourself as a leading figure in your catchment area. This process begins with a deep dive into the core of your professional identity, extracting the essence that sets you apart and packaging it in a manner that speaks directly to the hearts and minds of potential clients.

Your brand requires a clear understanding of what you stand for and should be a mirror reflecting your professional ethos, your approach to design, and the unique flair that marks your projects as unmistakably yours. This identity becomes your signature, a symbol of the quality and creativity that potential clients come to trust and seek out. These principles and values will guide your work and your interactions with clients, suppliers, and the community, making your brand relatable and showing your depth of character.

Your visual brand—encompassed in everything from your logo and colour scheme to the tone of your communications—should articulate what makes you different, better, and the preferred choice. This differentiation should be evident in your portfolio, where each project tells your story in your way of the challenges you met with innovative solutions you found, spaces transformed into oases of tranquillity and beauty, and clients' visions brought to life with your expertise and passion.

Your portfolio is the visual representation of your brand, the tangible proof of your capabilities and creativity. It should do more than display your projects; it should narrate each journey, explaining the challenges, the solutions, and the impact of the outcome. This storytelling approach adds layers to your portfolio that no one else has, making it a compelling tool for engagement. It invites potential clients into your world, showing them what you do and how and why you do it.

Consistency is the glue binding everything together. Every touchpoint should reinforce the same values, aesthetics, and commitment to quality. This consistency builds trust, a crucial commodity in a business where clients entrust you with their dreams and outdoor spaces.

Developing a visual personal brand is about positioning yourself as a provider of services, a creator of experiences, a weaver of dreams, and a trusted authority in your field. Be yourself, and don't try to be someone else. You can do a voice-over if you don't like being on camera in videos. Who will show up when someone hires you? Be that person. If you want to make a noise, do it.

When you have a personal brand, you can enjoy closing more projects; it's a weird feeling when a potential client thinks a celebrity is potentially coming to build them a water feature (because they have watched you on YouTube for hours). Some even say they can't wait to watch their pond being created on YouTube or Facebook.

Another benefit to a personal brand: Some clients would have stood over me before my videos. This was interesting as I started to film more and more; they would stay inside as they trusted me 100% to build their dream water feature. When you're creating aquatic art and want to avoid someone over your shoulder asking questions constantly, having a video link to send them can be a lifesaver; they don't even have to be yours. Knowing the video is out there or sharing a video of what they will likely be experiencing at that time or during the next stage is crucial, as is sharing the process of building a feature before you show up, which is a real game changer.

Sustainable Practices and Eco-Friendly Branding

Environmental awareness is appreciated and expected these days; integrating sustainable practices into your water feature projects and looking after your client and the planet is a must. This commitment to eco-friendliness speaks volumes about your brand's values, resonating deeply with a growing demographic of environmentally conscious clients. By prioritising sustainability, you position your brand as forward-thinking, responsible, and aligned with the global movement towards environmental preservation.

Today's consumers are more informed and concerned about the environmental impact of their choices than ever before. Show your dedication to sustainable practices, conserving water, using recycled materials where possible, and fostering the idea of working with Mother Nature. This commitment sets your brand apart and aligns it with the values of potential clients who prioritise sustainability in their landscaping choices.

Effectively communicating your sustainable practices is critical to captivating this eco-conscious audience. Transparency about your methods, materials, and the tangible benefits of an eco-friendly water feature can significantly enhance your appeal. Utilise your digital platforms, from your website to social media channels, to educate and engage with potential clients on the importance of sustainability. Share stories when your projects contribute to conservation efforts, highlight the long-term savings and ecological benefits, and showcase testimonials from satisfied clients who value your sustainable approach.

Education as a marketing tool can empower clients to make informed decisions aligned with their environmental values. Social media content and emails that offer insights into sustainable water feature design position you as a thought leader and build trust and credibility with your audience. This educational approach fosters a deeper connection with potential clients, encouraging them to choose your services for their meaningful impact on the environment.

Navigating Business Growth and Strategic Collaborations

As your garden water feature business flourishes, the challenge often lies not in the growth itself but in sustaining the unique quality and personal touch that sets your brand apart. Here are strategies for scaling your operations without diluting the essence of your brand, leveraging collaborations for mutual benefit.

Growth should never come at the cost of the characteristics that define your brand. Implementing scalable systems and processes is crucial to maintaining consistency in service quality, design excellence, and customer experience. Whether considering broadening your service offerings or exploring a larger catchment area, ensure that your brand's core values and design philosophy remain central to every decision.

Collaborating with like-minded professionals in your immediate area or related fields can significantly enhance your brand's growth and visibility. Such partnerships allow for the exchange of ideas, access to broader markets, and the opportunity to undertake more ambitious projects that might have needed to be more feasible.

Identifying and nurturing the right partnerships requires discernment and a clear understanding of your brand's long-term goals. Seek collaborators who bring complementary skills and a shared vision for quality, sustainability, and customer satisfaction. Remember, the right partnership can amplify your brand's strengths, push creative boundaries, and open up new avenues for growth.

Effective collaborations expand your brand's reach and create value for all stakeholders involved. Whether through joint marketing efforts, shared resources, or co-designed projects, strive for outcomes that benefit your brand and your partners. This approach enhances the project's success and strengthens the professional network within the pond and water feature industry, fostering a culture of innovation and mutual support.

Navigating business growth and collaborations requires a delicate balance between ambition and authenticity. By focusing on sustainable scaling, strategic partnerships, and maintaining the essence of your brand, you can ensure that your garden water feature business grows in size, value, and reputation. Remember, the goal is not just to build water features but to create lasting impressions and meaningful spaces that reflect the best of your brand's capabilities and vision.

Marketing Strategies

The ultimate aim of your marketing strategy should be a narrative that not only displays your technical ability and creative flair but also encapsulates the essence of what makes your brand unique. It's about creating a dialogue beyond the initial sale, fostering a community of enthusiasts and advocates for your business and the messages you put into the world.

Embracing the digital landscapes to sculpt a brand that resonates deeply with your desired clientele is a given these days. Effective marketing in this specialised industry involves showcasing your portfolio and narrating your vision or the story behind each water feature—transforming each project into a compelling invitation for potential clients.

Defining Your Target Market

Grasping the language of your ideal customer and what they are looking for long-term forms the foundation of your marketing endeavours. It's about tuning into their aspirations, preferences, and lifestyle choices to tailor your messaging. Utilise the digital prowess of social media and a well-curated website, and remember the use of selected printed copy to broadcast the uniqueness of your water feature designs. High-resolution professional-quality imagery paired with engaging narratives can captivate and connect, resulting in unparalleled growth and customer satisfaction.

Creating a User-Friendly Website

A website is your digital shop window, so its design should be inviting and functional. Key elements include easy navigation that guides visitors effortlessly through your services, a professional aesthetic that reflects your brand identity, and content that compellingly showcases your projects. This digital foundation solidifies your credibility and is a critical touchpoint for attracting business.

Your website should include critical information at the front and centre.

- **What services do you offer?**
  Is there enough information for visitors to understand what you offer and what you don't offer.
- **Who will be showing up?**
  Is there an About page with faces or videos about the process of hiring you and your team.
- **Where is your catchment area?**
  It's frustrating to find local trade people today. Does your website show where you work?

Local SEO (Search Engine Optimisation) effectively boosts your online presence and makes your brand more discoverable to those looking for water features in your area.

Choosing the Right Social Media Platforms

When choosing social media platforms to promote your work, you must consider where your target audience is most active. Platforms such as Facebook, Instagram and Pinterest, which rely heavily on visual content, are great for showcasing the impact of your work in a visually appealing way. To build a loyal following around your brand, it's crucial to actively engage with your community and create a sense of belonging. Engaging with your followers by responding to comments, asking for their opinions, and sharing user-generated content can help you build a strong community around your brand.

Content marketing is a great way to enhance your website by sharing your expertise. You can use standalone web pages and lead magnets, project profile videos, and infographics to create educational content that resonates with your audience. This can include design inspiration, maintenance tips, and information about the transformative power of water features. Mixing up your content by showcasing your projects, sharing educational posts, and giving behind-the-scenes glimpses into your work process is important.

Don't spread yourself too thin. If you like using one platform, master it and be consistent. Once you build up traction, you can expand. As the business grows, consider paying others or running campaigns, spending around 7-11% on marketing (as you can afford it). I recommend controlling and doing all the content yourself if you turn over less than 100K per year.

Exploring new marketing channels can significantly differentiate your brand. Augmented reality (AR) experiences that let customers visualise water features in their own spaces or drone videography that captures the grandeur of your projects from a bird's-eye view offer unique ways to captivate a tech-savvy audience. These innovative approaches not only engagingly showcase your work but also appeal to lots of demographics, setting your brand apart in a crowded market.

Email Marketing - Crafting Conversations, Not Campaigns

View each email as a conversation rather than a one-sided campaign. Invite feedback, ask questions, and encourage replies to transform your email list into an active community.

Creating a list of your contacts is recommended to ensure that you can reach your audience despite external digital changes you cannot control. You can still access your contacts if your social media account gets shut down. If your current community is small but active and stored on your phone, that's fine. However, it's essential to know who is who when building your email lists. As you grow, it's crucial to personalise your emails as much as possible. To do this, you will need software to manage your contacts effectively. This is where a CRM (Customer Relationship Management) comes into play. It will help you segment your audience and tailor your messages to customers' needs and interests. Getting people off your social media platforms or website to a list or CRM you own is vital.

Email marketing can significantly deepen customer engagement when executed with precision and genuine intent, converting passive observers into active participants in your brand's journey. By offering value, sharing knowledge, and creating a space for dialogue, you build a list and cultivate a community that champions your brand. This strategy nurtures leads and fosters a network of loyal clients and advocates, ensuring the longevity and vibrancy of your garden water feature business.

Email marketing is not just a tool but a crucial bridge between social media engagements and a more stable, controllable form of communication. Inviting people into a more intimate, personalised space. This transition safeguards your connection against the unpredictability of social media platforms.

Use the SLO Approach With Your Emails

Crafting emails that resonate involves more than broadcasting news; it's about storytelling that entices, educates, and extends offers that feel personalised and valuable.

Story (S): Share behind-the-scenes glimpses, day-to-day success stories, or the inspiration behind a particular design. These stories foster a deeper emotional connection; information with emotion is retained, making your brand more relatable and memorable. The number of people that react to your content if you can shock or hook them is incredible.

Lesson (L): Impart knowledge gained from the story, whether it's maintenance tips, design principles, or the benefits of eco-friendly water features—educational content positions you as an expert, building trust and authority.

Offer (O): While not every email should sell, strategic offers tailored to the recipient's interests can drive engagement and conversions. These could include exclusive deals, early access to new products or features, or invitations to private pond tours.

By creating well-crafted email campaigns, you can nurture leads into loyal clients. Entice website visitors and social media followers to subscribe by offering compelling incentives. This could be an exclusive ebook on creating sanctuaries in the garden, access to video tutorials on how to clean or upgrade their features, or a way to book a free consultation/discovery call.

Embracing Digital Transformation
Utilising social media to showcase projects and share expert advice is just the beginning. Digital tools like project management software can streamline operations, while design tools enhance the project planning phase. Customer relationship management (CRM) systems improve client interactions, ensuring a smooth experience from initial consultation to project completion. These digital solutions improve efficiency and enable a higher level of service, reinforcing your brand's commitment to excellence and innovation.

Online Reviews and Reputation Management
Online reviews significantly influence trust and credibility. Actively encourage satisfied clients to share their experiences online and employ strategies for

managing your digital reputation. This includes responding to negative feedback constructively and showcasing your commitment to customer satisfaction and your brand's integrity.

Measuring Success: Analytics, Feedback, Adjustments

Leveraging analytics tools enables you to track the effectiveness of your digital marketing strategies, from website traffic patterns to email campaign open rates. Use this data to make informed decisions, continually adjusting your approach based on direct feedback and performance metrics to optimise your online presence and marketing efforts.

Customer Experience and Storytelling

Utilising storytelling can profoundly enhance your brand, allowing for a more emotional and memorable connection with your audience. The customer experience journey, from the first point of contact through post-installation maintenance, is an opportunity to live out and reinforce your brand values. Each interaction is a chapter in a story that reflects the quality of your work and the essence of your brand identity. By weaving compelling narratives around your projects—highlighting challenges overcome, client testimonials, and the transformative power of your water features—you embed your brand in the hearts and minds of your audience.

Buying Back Your Time

Instead of answering customer questions over the phone 1 to 1, why not have Q&A as part of your marketing? If one person has the question, others do, too. Use social media to get ideas of what people are searching for and answer questions to get in front of customers in your local market. My trade customers say that social media wastes time or this platform is for kids.

It's a genuine concern everyone on your social media platforms might not buy from you, but it's not a waste of your time as you start to understand what your people need and the information and stories they are attracted to.

Mastering social media platforms to showcase the beauty and intricacy of water in someone's garden is fantastic. If it's engaging content and you find interactive posts, get the post out to your local market and website visitors. You want to build a loyal local community, significantly boosting your brand's visibility and driving customer engagement.

One person who has mastered this on Facebook is my good friend Gerard Touhey. He loves to laugh and make people laugh with his use of wigs and his favourite drinks as an Irishman (Guinness and Jameson). His use of bright colours is all around his personality, so you can bet that when he finishes a feature, it includes one, if not all, of the things he loves. The Happy Crazy Irish Pond Builder entertains his audience with outlandish stuff, from his open garden tours to his beautiful garden. I love his bowls, overflowing with joy and surrounded by lovely moss.

Be careful. I want to put out a warning: as you have read, you will attract more of what you post on social media. Years ago, wanting to make as much noise as possible and trying to put out daily posts, I would post about anything and everything.

This is a good strategy as they are all touchpoints, but if you are doing stuff just simply paying the bills, like a singer, you will need to do what you can while waiting for the next gig. I was posting about me simply relining traditional ponds. I wanted these features to be better designed, which would last and not turn back into leaking holes in people's gardens. I wanted better opportunities, something other than this long-term. I wanted to showcase aquatic art, which is a little more work, but the story was huge, changing how ponds were built.

I stopped relining and started re-building with my style. Bingo, I began to attract my kind of customers and started to create a brand. Only put out what you want to attract. Build it, and they will come.

Are you facing marketing challenges? Encouraging clients to share their experiences and photos of your water features on your business Google listing will increase local organic growth as Google loves activity and enhance brand credibility without significant advertising spend. Even if you get a 1-star review, how you respond will help no end. I got a 1-star review once, and I thought it was the end of the world; it turned out it was fake. The person was trying to be funny, saying I had caused his fish to drown, so I thought, how can I start making lemonade from the lemon?

I created a YouTube video explaining that pond fish can drown, educating my viewers on the importance of oxygen and that it's the biggest killer of fish after stress.

Developing Your Brand and Marketing Strategy

Crafting a distinctive brand and a compelling marketing strategy involves four crucial steps:

- **Brand Identity**
  Identify what sets you apart. This could be your unique design philosophy, commitment to sustainability, or exceptional customer service. Ensure your brand identity is consistently reflected across all your marketing materials.
- **Content Strategy**
  Develop a content strategy that showcases your expertise and highlights the beauty and functionality of your water features. This could include blog posts, how-to guides, and behind-the-scenes looks at your projects.
- **Social Media Engagement**
  Choose platforms that align with your target audience and utilise them to share your work, engage with followers, and build a community around your brand. Regular interaction and authentic content will foster deeper connections.

- **Analytics and Adjustment**
  Use analytics to monitor the performance of your marketing initiatives. Pay attention to what resonates with your audience and adjust your strategies to maximise effectiveness. Once you find what works, spend money and use this content in local adverts to attract your local market.

By understanding and applying all these strategies, principles, and techniques, you can enhance your digital footprint, forge deeper connections with your audience and cultivate a business that thrives on innovation, customer loyalty and satisfaction, and sustained brand recognition. Success in aquatics is about more than just the quality of your water features. It's about effectively communicating your brand and engaging with your market.

7

SALES TECHNIQUES AND CUSTOMER RELATIONSHIPS

This chapter will be your compass, guiding you through the intricate landscapes of sales and customer relationships. Using proven strategies and insights from industry leaders like Tim Cutroni, we will ensure that your path to sales success and customer satisfaction is clear and achievable.

Communicating the value of your services and turning potential clients into long-term, loyal customers can take time. Water features are not bought—they are sold, so buckle up; this chapter is good.

The Art of Selling and Relationship Building

Tim Cutroni from New England Aquatic Landscaping and The Contractor Fight is a wordsmith and a master at sales. His sales success stems from the power of building relationships quickly. He is building a legacy with his family and creating ripples in the sales world. He is a testament to personal growth, transforming his approach to connect deeply with clients' desires rather than just focusing on the technical aspects.

Tim is not a pond guy, so it is about more than just the quality of work. He loves people, and it's about how you engage with clients, share knowledge, and continuously provide value, crafting a business that changes lives, has fun, and forges lasting relationships.

One example was when he introduced weekly pond tips via email, what we call "weekly touchpoints". Touchpoints not only revive dormant leads but also solidify your position as the go-to pond expert for your customers.

Since 2015, I have been talking to Tim weekly. Over the years, Tim has helped me and has been a vital part of The Pond Advisor Network. It takes a mastermind (many minds coming together) to understand and develop sales techniques and value propositions (how a product or service solves customers' problems or improves their situation, delivering specific benefits). Combined with genuine relationship-building efforts, this is crucial for long-term success.

Surround yourself with people who have what you want. This might be a mindset that needs to be continuously improved. It is beneficial to have someone to help, challenge, and refine your sales approach and ways to invest in client relationships and the customer life cycle (stages a customer goes through when considering, purchasing, using, and maintaining loyalty to a product or service).

To effectively communicate the value and vision behind your approach to sales, I want you to take the information and make it your own. There are many ways to sell, and your way might differ from mine; that's okay. I am open-minded and would love it if you were too during this chapter. I could write a whole book on this and still leave stuff on the table.

This section is based on Tim's approach, which focuses on the client's desires and blends sales with the art of relationship building.

For water feature professionals, identifying and effectively communicating your Unique Selling Points (USPs) is critical. USPs are those particular services or attributes that make your offerings stand out. For Tim, it wasn't just the water features but the process of understanding what the client truly desired, turning sales conversations into a deeply personal service. Tim's customers don't buy lights. They buy nighttime illumination.

Your USPs simplify the decision-making process for clients by highlighting the benefits of your service. This clarity is instrumental in justifying yourself (as if you are only partially sold on the silver and gold moments you are selling). You might be selling aquatic art or a water feature. However, you are selling time, time people would not ordinarily have with themselves, friends or family. All we have is time; be careful of how you use it! How do you put a price on time? If you don't value it, you cannot sell or price it and foster client loyalty. Tim's method of sending weekly pond tips via email exemplifies this—by continuously providing and highlighting the value and establishing himself as the go-to expert, he re-engages dormant leads and cements his reputation and client trust.

You must always seek the client's consent before proceeding with the sales process or taking specific actions. So, with that, let's move on.

Sales Techniques

Sales techniques and scripts are essential tools for any contractor. They provide a framework for engaging potential clients, addressing their concerns, and guiding them towards making decisions.

Thorough client consultations are pivotal in understanding their motives, desires, concerns, and expectations for your water feature projects. This process ensures a deep alignment between your services and the client's vision, setting a solid foundation for satisfaction and trust.

The idea is for you to talk about 30% of the time during a phone consultation, so ask a question and then shut your mouth. You must demonstrate how your services uniquely address the client's requirements and vision. However, you want them to talk.

Customise your sales pitches and use your words. Here is an example of how I have customised a simple word. I don't like the word "honest" when used in a sales conversation: "Can I be honest with you?", as it implies to me the person saying it has not always been honest. Some salespeople like using the word "candid" instead of "honest", but I still don't like this word. I have a problem with the terminology. I spent a long time thinking about a different way of saying the same thing and came up with the word "straightforward", which is my customisation: "Can I be straightforward with you?". You might think I am going too deep, but some clients will also be if I am thinking this. I have tested this several times.

Here are some practical questions to help your sales pitches:

- How long have you wanted this? *Why now?*
- Have you ever done a project like this?
- What questions can I answer? *I want to know how I can best help you.*
- What don't you like about your water feature?
- What have you tried to fix this? *Did that work?*

Please note: If your prospects keep asking you multiple questions at a time, you need to be careful; they might just be picking your brains. In this example, I reply, "If I hear you right, it sounds like you're after a consulting service." Another reply is, "Instead of boiling down the information here, let me send you a link to a video or article which will be able to help better."

If a prospect keeps looping around to, "Just come out to see us", this might also be someone trying to get free information; stick to your process. If you need the experience of going out to understand the situation, then do it. Soon, you will not need to jump in a vehicle to understand what's happening. Value your time because if you don't, who does? Charge for an on-site consultation (a whole topic in itself).

My reply to someone who keeps asking about me coming out: "Yes, that would be a great idea. Let's do this before I come out for an on-site design consultation or to carry out a pre-job walkthrough. Have I answered all your questions, as I can help over the phone?"

If you have answered all the questions, this could be an excellent time to talk about money, so ask permission first.

"I believe I have a solution; can I share with you what others have looked at before in this situation?" or "I have several options for you" (Give them the high option before the low option).

"Which makes the most sense to talk about first?"

"Whereabouts are you in this process?"

That's a lot of money. "A lot more money?" Mirroring will prompt the prospect to explain.

Make a list of your questions and practice with friends and family. If you have peers, it's even better, as you can practise both sides with pictures.

Practising Your Sales Process

While "role-playing" might be off-putting for some, I like to rebrand it as a "practice run", which can make the exercise more palatable.

Why should you practise?

All athletes practise to stay at the top of their game and be match-fit. Professional athletes have coaches and managers who help them focus on the fundamentals needed to win. Contractors must be match-fit or ready to talk to someone who wants to pay them for their services.

Practising your sales processes will build your confidence as this reduces anxiety and highlights words you will use automatically, helping your ability to handle different types of customer interactions. Regular practice helps refine your messaging (learning word tracks or scripts), ensuring you effectively communicate your services' value. By working through various scenarios, you can better tailor your approach to meet each prospect's specific needs and concerns.

Writing a Compelling Proposal

A well-presented proposal reflects the quality and professionalism of your work. The format and the way you present your proposal does matter. Use a professional software system, ensure no typos or grammatical errors, and brand your proposal with your logo and colour scheme.

If you can present the proposal in person, it's much better. Then, you can talk the customer through the benefits. I used to take a mobile printer with me on design consultations before people started to do bank transfers. I would let the customers know I would write the proposal in the van. This would also allow the customers some alone time (as it takes 10-15 minutes) so they can talk before I ask for a deposit.

It's always best to collect deposits with clients in their gardens; you can video a pre-job walkthrough so everyone is on the same page. Agreeing on the scope of work, give them the prices and walk them through your payment options.

We have a few options for projects running over a few days.

We offer a 10% prepay discount option, which allows us to collect 100% of the money—well, 90% after we take off the discount. This is only available on the day or beforehand if clients want to lock in prices (any change orders are also fully paid upfront).

The next option is 50% down, and the balance when 100% happy. Then last but not least, first deposit of 33%, then the next 33% payment once we both agree and book a start date, and finally, the balance when 100% happy. We say balance, as sometimes we have change orders during the construction process.

If prospects want to consider the options, we only invoice for the consultation fee, offering the rest of the deposit back so we can concentrate on moving forward. However, we always schedule a follow-up to discuss any questions or concerns the client may have. This shows your dedication to your project and allows you to address any hesitations they might have.

Better Proposals

Understand Your Client's Needs

Begin by deeply understanding the client's vision. This empathy, a hallmark of Tim's approach, ensures your proposal speaks directly to their dreams and concerns.

Clarity and Conciseness

Use straightforward language to describe your services and the project scope. Clear communication prevents misunderstandings and builds confidence.

Visuals

Incorporate links to videos explaining the process or photos to help clients visualise the outcome. Compelling visuals can be incredibly persuasive in an industry where aesthetics play a crucial role.

Detail the Work

Outline each project phase, including design concepts and material choices. Setting clear expectations lays the groundwork for a smooth project execution.

Highlight USPs

Articulate what makes your services unique, whether it's your innovative design approach, sustainability practices, or unmatched craftsmanship.

Include Testimonials
Sharing experiences from satisfied clients can significantly enhance your proposal's credibility.

Timeline and Budget
Provide a realistic timeline and transparent budget breakdown, demonstrating your commitment to honesty and integrity.

Aftercare Services
Outline the maintenance and care services you offer post-completion, showcasing your long-term commitment to the project and client satisfaction.

Leveraging Customer Loyalty

Focus on building loyalty once you've converted a sceptical prospect into a customer. Excellent after-sales service, regular check-ins, and ongoing support ensure satisfaction and encourage referrals and repeat business. Engage with customers through newsletters, maintenance tips, and updates on new services to keep your brand in their minds.

Transforming scepticism into loyalty is about listening, understanding, and responding effectively to your prospects' concerns. By demonstrating empathy, flexibility, and a commitment to excellence, you can build a solid customer base that believes in the value of your services and the beauty of your water features.

Educate and Inform

Use objections as teachable moments. Provide detailed information, share success stories, and even offer private pond tours to existing installations to educate prospects about the benefits and feasibility of water features. Sometimes, it's even better to have unguided tours or displays. This was why I installed several features in my front garden. This also gives clients an option for a free next step, as we always charge for our time when going to their gardens.

Offer Custom Solutions

Emphasise the customisation of your services. Show how you can design a water feature that meets their needs, concerns, and preferences, underscoring your commitment to delivering personalised value. We offer packages, but no-two-water features are the same when building out of rock, and every location is different.

Build Credibility

Share satisfied customer testimonials, reviews, and case studies. Seeing real-life examples of your work and positive feedback from others can significantly reduce scepticism. Suppose you can get prospects to other customers' homes. This is the top benefit as the homeowners become your sales staff as they love their water features and understand the value.

Guarantee Satisfaction

Offer guarantees or warranties for your work to alleviate fears of investment risk. This demonstrates confidence in your services and commitment to quality. We offer a 12-month no-quibble guarantee on all our aquatic art. We looked at providing a lifetime guarantee, provided we were in charge of the maintenance.

Follow Up

Persistence is key. Follow up with prospects after initial discussions to address any lingering doubts, offer additional information, or propose a revised solution. No answer is not a "NO"; email and update them until people tell you to stop or say "No, thank you".

Addressing Concerns and Objections

Recognising that objections are often rooted in a lack of information or understanding rather than outright disinterest. They provide an opportunity to further engage with the prospect by clarifying concerns and demonstrating value.

Cost Concerns

Many prospects might want you to improve the price of installing and maintaining a garden water feature. Looking for a deal, I have found these clients can become a nightmare. If you give an inch, they take a mile. If they might be shocked by the price, give them time to justify it themselves. Reply, "I can imagine how frustrated you might be; what were you hoping to hear?" If you end up miles apart, ask them, "What do you think we should do next?"

Wanting a Breakdown

This could be an alarm that they want to beat you up with your pricing. It's okay to refuse if this is your process. Ask, "What will happen if I break down the price for you?" Many people need or want extra information, so return to the long-term value or highlight the benefit. It could be the potential value increase for the property or the saleability, the environmental benefits, and the personal enjoyment of a beautiful, serene space.

Maintenance Worries

Maintaining a pond can be daunting. Overcome this by explaining the simplicity of modern maintenance practices, offering maintenance plans, and showcasing how eco-friendly designs reduce upkeep. Most water features will require less maintenance if designed properly than a lawn or flower bed. Most of the maintenance is around the feature.

Space and Practicality
Prospects may need more space or the right environment. Combat this by presenting creative solutions tailored to small or challenging spaces, demonstrating your versatility and problem-solving skills. You don't have to use a small space for water in your garden. A large patio pond in a small space has a huge impact.

Fostering Long-Term Relationships
Exceeding client expectations is not just about delivering a project; it's about creating a memorable and positive experience that resonates with clients long after the work is completed. This approach fosters lasting relationships and solidifies your brand's reputation.

Building Trust and Credibility
High-quality work and attention to detail demonstrate your commitment to excellence, helping to establish trust and credibility with your clients. This reassures clients they've made the right choice in selecting your services, fostering a positive perception of your brand.

Enhancing Reputation
Satisfied clients are more likely to share their positive experiences with others through word-of-mouth or online

reviews. This can significantly boost your reputation, attracting more clients looking for proven quality and reliability.

Encourage Repeat Business
Clients who have exceeded their expectations are more likely to return for additional services. Repeat business is more cost-effective regarding marketing spend and helps build a loyal client base.

Mitigate Complaints and Negative Feedback
Focusing on quality and proactive communication reduces the likelihood of misunderstandings and dissatisfaction that can lead to complaints. Addressing potential issues before they escalate shows clients that their satisfaction is your priority.

Differentiate Your Business
In a competitive market, exceeding expectations can set your business apart. It highlights your unique value proposition and can position your brand as the preferred choice among consumers seeking superior service and outcomes.

Facilitate Upselling and Cross-Selling Opportunities
Clients who trust your commitment to excellence are more open to additional services or upgrade recommendations.

Building Strong Customer Relationships

The end of a project is just as critical as the beginning. The last 10% of the project is what clients are likely to remember the most. Ensuring that this final phase leaves nothing for the customer to do but enjoy their new water feature can significantly impact their overall satisfaction and the likelihood of them recommending your services to others.

Focus on the Finish

Make sure every project ends well. Complete all tasks, no matter how small, and ensure the site is clean and beautifully presented.

Personal Touch

Adding a personal touch, such as a thank-you note or a small gift (be actively looking for their favourite tipple—recycling bins are an excellent place to look for clues), can leave a great lasting impression.

Responsive Service

Highlight the importance of responsive service after completing the project. Quick and effective responses to any issues or queries that arise after the project is completed can significantly impact client trust and satisfaction.

Aftercare Support and Client Education

Client education can be beneficial throughout the whole process, from the sales call to the final walkthrough. Offer guidance on how they can enjoy and care for their water feature. Providing clear instructions and being available for follow-up questions reinforces your commitment to their satisfaction. Also, educating clients on their choices' ecological and aesthetic benefits can increase their appreciation and satisfaction with their features.

Engaging After Project Completion

Maintaining relationships with clients after project completion is critical to building a loyal customer base and encouraging repeat business and referrals.

Here are some key strategies to incorporate into your business:

Follow-Up Calls

A simple yet effective strategy, follow-up calls demonstrate your ongoing commitment to customer satisfaction. A casual visit to check on the water feature can turn clients into friends and advocates for your brand. Schedule these calls a few weeks after project completion to ensure everything is to the customer's liking and address any concerns they may have.

Warranty Reminders

As the warranty period draws close, remind your clients via email or a personal call. This shows you're proactive about their investment's longevity and opens the door to discussing any additional services they might need.

Email Updates

Regular email updates can keep your clients informed about maintenance tips, new services, or seasonal care reminders. Tailoring content to your clientele's seasons or specific needs adds value and keeps your brand at the forefront of your mind.

Leveraging Testimonials, Referrals and Reviews

Encouraging word-of-mouth from satisfied clients to share their experiences can significantly enhance your brand's visibility and credibility. At the end of the project, ask (a direct request can be very effective) if they would be willing to share their experience publicly and direct them to where they can do so. Personalise this request to make it feel more genuine and less like a standard procedure.

I have asked clients what helped them decide to purchase, especially when satisfaction is the highest at the end of a project. Reducing the effort required to leave a review increases the likelihood that they will do so.

Offer incentives for clients who take the time to share their experiences.

Satisfaction Surveys

Satisfaction surveys also provide valuable insights for improving your services and engaging the customer in your quality assurance process.

Customer Appreciation Parties

Hosting a customer appreciation party or a similar event can strengthen relationships with past clients. It's a gesture that shows gratitude and fosters a community among your clientele. These events provide an excellent opportunity for word-of-mouth marketing, as satisfied customers are likely to share their positive experiences with others.

Community Building

Building a community among your clients, such as social media groups where they can share their experiences, tips, and photos. This keeps your brand active in their lives and fosters a sense of belonging among clients. Encourage clients to share their stories and experiences with their water feature on your platform. This not only gives them a voice but also provides authentic, relatable content for your marketing efforts. Highlight positive reviews and testimonials on your website and social media channels. Seeing their featured feedback can make clients feel valued and encourage others to share their experiences.

Invitations to Feature on Tours or Showcases

Offer clients the chance to have their water feature showcased on tours; in your marketing materials, create content that clients are proud to share, such as photos or videos of their completed projects. Tagging clients in these posts (with their permission) on social media makes sharing with their network easy. This highlights their investment and positions them as proud partners in your work. It's a win-win that offers recognition for them and promotional content for you. Actively engage with clients who mention your brand on social media. Reposting their content (with permission), commenting, and thanking them for their shout-outs can encourage continued engagement and sharing.

Exclusive Offers

Provide past clients exclusive offers on future maintenance, upgrades, or new services. Tailoring these offers to their past projects can make the proposal more appealing and personal.

What's next?

- Identify your unique selling points and integrate them into your sales conversations.
- Implement a consistent follow-up strategy to keep your business top-of-mind for clients.
- Develop a loyalty program that rewards clients for their business and referrals.
- Train in active listening and empathy to effectively handle objections and concerns.

"Take charge of your circumstances and strive towards happiness. Winners make it happen; losers let it happen."

8
PROJECT MANAGEMENT AND OPERATIONS

You might have built a reputable business from scratch, but as your reputation grows alongside the demand for custom, one-of-a-kind water features, you will be faced with a new challenge or crossroads.

Dealing with the increasing complexity and scale of projects on your own, you may find yourself moving from smaller, manageable tasks to more extensive and intricate installations. This chapter is dedicated to exploring tailored solutions and strategies to help solopreneurs like you scale your operations, manage client expectations, and streamline project workflows without losing the essence of what makes your work unique.

Embarking on a project management and operations journey in the water feature industry can be intimidating, especially for a solopreneur. The creative allure of designing and constructing water features is familiar territory, but project management may seem less so. However, this chapter lays a solid foundation for realising your artistic vision without compromising quality, budget, or timeline.

Managing projects as a solo business owner presents unique challenges and opportunities. Without a traditional team, the weight of numerous responsibilities rests solely on your shoulders. Efficiency goes beyond achieving a work-life balance; it's crucial for transitioning your business from mere survival to a thriving enterprise.

This chapter aims to demystify the complexities of project management, providing practical strategies and solutions explicitly crafted for solopreneurs in the water feature industry.

We will cover:

Streamlined Planning and Scheduling
Learn how to map out your projects effectively, ensuring timely completion without overlooking any detail.

Quality Assurance

Discover methods to maintain and elevate the quality of your installations, ensuring each project meets or exceeds both client expectations and industry standards.

Effective Client Communication

Gain insights into building strong relationships with your clients through proactive and transparent communication, which is essential for project success and repeat business.

Risk Management

Understand how to identify potential risks early on and develop strategies to mitigate them, keeping your projects on track and within budget.

Tools for Success

Explore user-friendly project management software and tools that can simplify your workflow, allowing you to focus on the creative aspects of your projects.

As you read further, you will find insights on how to manage the entire project lifecycle single-handedly while preparing for future expansion. This chapter is not only instructional but also inspirational, promising to equip you with the knowledge to bring your aquatic dreams to life with precision, excellence, and unparalleled satisfaction for your clients. Let it be the cornerstone of your journey toward building a lasting legacy in the water feature industry.

In the early days of being a sole trader, I faced several challenges: a lack of money, excessive stress, long hours away from home, material delays, and even court cases, which resulted in dissatisfied clients and me dropping the ball. Clients would call me at all hours of the day. To stay organised, I had to-do lists and Post-it notes everywhere. One even made me laugh as it had a line item to finish my to-do lists. I then adopted a "daily power list" with a few questions for me to answer.

Did I win the day yesterday?
- [ ] Yes
- [ ] No

Did I fill out the power list for yesterday?
- [ ] Yes
- [ ] No

How much actual money did I make yesterday? This is different from the turnover, it's the money I can pay myself with.

I soon realised that I needed more structure and project management principles. I began using project management software after learning what to charge and implementing practical management strategies with my mentor's help. It took me three years of focused work to improve project planning, monitoring, and communication. However, it resulted in easier project management, more word-of-mouth referrals, repeat business, and a better work-life balance. I was happier and had greater personal fulfilment on the job site.

Streamlining for Efficiency as a Solopreneur

For the solopreneur navigating the intricate world of water feature installation, streamlining operations is not just a luxury—it's necessary for thriving in an industry that demands precision and creativity. This section delves into practical, accessible strategies designed to weave efficiency into the very fabric of your solo venture, enhancing project outcomes without compromising the personal touch that sets your brand apart.

Streamlining Project Workflows
Understanding the need for a straightforward approach to project management, consider adopting simple yet powerful tools that dovetail seamlessly with your unique workflow. Whether it's leveraging intuitive project management software that resonates with your solo operations or utilising custom spreadsheets, the goal is to

keep your projects, deadlines, and tasks in a cohesive, easily manageable format. This approach not only sharpens your organisational edge but also allows you to concentrate on what truly matters—crafting exquisite water features and nurturing client relationships.

Simplifying Operations with Standard Procedures

The power of standard operating procedures (SOPs) cannot be overstated, especially when each project you undertake is a testament to your craftsmanship. By establishing clear, straightforward SOPs for your most frequented tasks—from initial site assessment to the final touches of installation—you lay the groundwork for consistency and excellence across all your projects.

This not only streamlines your process, saving invaluable time, but also reassures your clients of the unwavering quality they can expect from your hands. As you grow, these SOPs become the blueprint for any team members you might bring on board, ensuring they align perfectly with your vision and standards.

Embracing Lean Principles in Solo Operations

Often perceived as the domain of more significant operations, lean principles can be remarkably transformative for the solopreneur. Start by critically assessing your current processes to identify any inefficiencies, such as how you manage your materials or redundant steps that sneak into your installation procedures.

The objective is simple—eliminate waste and optimise every resource. This lean approach enhances the efficiency of your operations and elevates the quality of your projects, ensuring you deliver unmatched value to your clients. Embracing a culture of continuous improvement, you'll find yourself constantly looking for ways to refine and elevate your service offering.

By integrating these streamlined practices into your day-to-day operations, you not only set the stage for enhanced productivity and reduced overhead but also create an environment where quality and client satisfaction are the hallmarks of your business. Whether you remain a one-person show or aspire to grow your operation, these principles are your stepping stones to a flourishing future in the water feature industry.

Efficiency and Time Management

For solopreneurs in the water feature industry, mastering the art of time management and operational efficiency isn't just about keeping a tight schedule; it's about crafting a workflow that allows for the seamless realisation of your projects with less stress and more satisfaction.

Here are some practical strategies to enhance your daily operations and project execution:

Optimising Daily Operations with Time Management
Initiate each day with a clear plan. Utilising digital tools, such as a calendar app, can help you allocate specific blocks of time to various tasks, including on-site work, administrative duties, and travel. This structured approach ensures you're making the most of each day, keeping you on track and focused on your goals.

When I was on my own, I would start big projects on a Monday and aim to work on a job site for three or four days a week, with Thursday and Friday as my office days. If I had weather issues, I would change the admin or office day to that day. This also helps with hiring subcontractor labourers (Monday - Wednesday). You know you would be on the job site three days a week. Plus, you could book them weeks in advance and they know when you need them, week on week.

Strategic Task Prioritisation
Identifying and tackling high-priority tasks early ensures that your energy is directed towards activities with the highest impact on your project's success. Distinguishing between urgent tasks and those that are truly important can help you navigate your to-do list more effectively,

ensuring critical deadlines are met, and progress is continuous.

The framework we use is to split the day into four 90-minute sections when not on the job site, and then we follow the step-by-step process of the task. We call these sessions:

F1 is Important - Urgent
F2 is Important - Not Urgent
F3 is Urgent - Not Important
F4 is Not Urgent - Not Important

I use the letter "F" to represent each 90-minute slot, symbolising Focus. This helps me highlight the significance of directing my attention and resources towards specific tasks that align with my strategic goals. By doing so, I can enhance productivity, make better decisions, and reduce stress—especially in managing and growing my business.

Elevating Quality and Nurturing Client Relationships

For solopreneurs in the water feature industry, the twin pillars of quality control and client communication are not just operational tasks but the essence of building a trusted brand. Emphasising these elements can significantly enhance client satisfaction, fostering a business environment ripe for repeat engagements and glowing referrals.

Quality Control: Your Signature of Excellence

As a solopreneur, every project you undertake reflects your dedication to excellence. Implementing stringent quality control measures throughout the project lifecycle ensures that each water feature not only aligns with industry standards but also exceeds client expectations. This commitment to quality, manifested through regular inspections, responsive feedback implementation, and proactive adjustments, solidifies your reputation as a detail-oriented professional. This unwavering commitment reassures clients of your reliability, encouraging their trust and setting a high benchmark for your services.

Mastering Client Communication: The Art of Connection

Effective communication is the thread that weaves through the fabric of each project, binding your vision to your client's dreams. Establishing a rhythm of regular updates, transparent conversations, and proactive engagements ensures your clients feel valued and involved. This dialogue continues after project completion.

Still, it extends to thorough handover sessions where clients are walked through their new aquatic masterpiece, ensuring they are content and genuinely enchanted. Offering comprehensive care instructions underscores your dedication to their long-term satisfaction, leaving an indelible mark of professionalism.

Harmonising Expectations and Collaborations

Setting clear expectations and maintaining open channels with suppliers and collaborators are crucial practices for solo water feature specialists. Transparent discussions about project capabilities within set budgets and timelines prevent misunderstandings and foster a climate of trust. Keeping meticulous records of project communications and decisions aids in navigating any challenges, ensuring that every party's contributions align seamlessly towards the project's success.

For the solo water feature installer, balancing quality control with effective client communication is not merely a strategy but a philosophy that defines every project. By embedding these practices into your workflow, you cultivate a business that thrives on trust, quality, and the personal touch that distinguishes your brand in the marketplace.

This approach ensures project success and lays the groundwork for a flourishing business buoyed by satisfied clients and a growing portfolio of mesmerising water features. You want to talk to them instead of hiring or being overwhelmed when the phone rings.

Navigating the Waters of Risk and Challenge Management

Before diving into the intricate world of project management tools and the art of streamlining operations, solopreneurs in the water feature industry must grasp the significance of preemptive risk management. This section lays the foundation for understanding how anticipating and mitigating potential issues is instrumental in navigating the unpredictable currents of water feature projects.

Risk Management Strategies

In the nuanced field of garden water feature projects, adept risk management is not just advisable—it's imperative. This involves a systematic process of identifying potential risks—be it physical, financial, or operational—assessing their probable impact and crafting strategies to mitigate them effectively.

Recognising risks early in the planning phase allows professionals to develop comprehensive mitigation plans. These plans might include contingencies for supply chain disruptions, strategies for handling unexpected ground conditions, and protocols for managing client-driven changes. By prioritising risk management, water feature professionals can ensure project resilience, maintain budget control, and uphold client satisfaction, ultimately steering projects toward seamless completion.

Mastering risk management is an essential skill, especially for those flying solo. It involves the meticulous identification and analysis of potential obstacles that could derail your project—unforeseen ground conditions, supply chain hiccups, or shifts in client vision. Early identification and strategic planning can arm you with the necessary contingencies to keep your project on track and within budget, ensuring resilience against the unexpected.

Tackling Common Risks Head-On
Unexpected Ground Conditions
Encountering unforeseen ground conditions, such as buried utilities or unstable soil, can delay projects and inflate costs. Unexpected subterranean surprises can escalate costs and delay timelines. Proactive strategies, such as conducting thorough site assessments pre-project and securing clear contingencies in your quotes, can

safeguard against such unpredictabilities. Remember, transparency and flexibility in dealing with discovered obstacles, like hidden concrete or utilities, can turn potential setbacks into opportunities for creative problem-solving.

What you can control: Vanguard against unforeseen circumstances during the consultation phase and again on the pre-job walkthrough. This preemptive approach allows for the adjustment of plans and understanding of budgets before encountering any surprises.

You often dig up or find items or concrete. I always add this line or something to this effect in our quotes.

> "Conditions beyond our control, such as moving buried services, correcting existing drainage problems, or removing below-ground debris, will require separate labour charges when necessary."

We will discuss changing the design or layout if we find any concrete or unexpected extra work. If there are any additional costs, they should be agreed upon in writing before any extra work starts. I use the line "We need a change order, or we can do this within the agreed budget".

I remember one waterfall I found with seven different concrete and cement layers. It was causing issues once I spoke to the customer and showed the different ways; we changed the plan and had the waterfall built on the other side of the pond so we could leave the rockery and budget in place, and the waterfall would look much more natural.

Supply Chain Stability

Delays in the delivery or availability of materials such as machinery, skips, stones and dry goods can all stall projects and impact schedules. The reliability of material delivery is pivotal. Cultivating strong supplier relationships and maintaining a keen eye on inventory levels ensures you're prepared for supply chain disruptions. Proactively securing materials upon project confirmation minimises the risk of delays, keeping your projects flowing smoothly.

What you can control: Build strong relationships with suppliers. Using the same ones, often loyalty, goes a long way. As soon as you receive deposits, talk to your suppliers to secure the stock and pay for it if needed. I maintain a buffer stock and find that if I have items in stock, I am more likely to sell them. It's not always possible to keep materials in stock due to space or logistics. If you talk to the vendor once you have money for the job or if it takes longer than you first thought, ask them to stay informed about potential supply chain issues.

Years ago, it was more challenging when I was the first contractor installing Aquascape Inc. gear. At one point, I was selling spaces (I had 10 features sold, waiting for materials). So, I implemented flexible project start dates and communicated transparently with clients about potential issues.

Client-Driven Changes

Changes in project scopes or designs the client requests during construction can lead to increased costs and extended timelines. The dynamic nature of client preferences necessitates a robust framework for managing changes. Establishing clear communication channels from the get-go, complemented by detailed contracts anticipating the need for adjustments, empowers you to navigate changes with agility. This approach maintains project integrity and nurtures client trust, laying the groundwork for a partnership built on mutual respect and understanding.

What you can control: As soon as you establish clear communication channels and set client expectations. Use detailed contracts and quotes on more significant projects. It's common to include clauses for change orders outlining the process for handling changes, including approval mechanisms, cost adjustments, and impact on timelines. Address concerns early and adapt plans as needed: people change their minds (which is okay), and some people have the money to change it often. If you want to offer this seven-star service, you should charge for it. I have given deposits back to high-profile individuals and pulled off jobs until artistic freedom was given. You are a professional; you will face clients in the early days asking to move stuff around and be involved in the project. Be warned, as I warn my clients, if we move this (say stone) and you prefer it where it was in the first place, it will incur extra fees to push them back. If you order materials for a project and the client changes their mind, stocking and handling fees can be charged (look into your rights).

By proactively addressing these common risks, you can minimise disruptions, maintain client satisfaction, and ensure the smooth completion of projects.

Overcoming Other Project Challenges
Weathering the Storms
The unpredictable British weather demands a flexible approach to scheduling and project execution. Transparent communication with your clients about the impact of weather on timelines and quality is essential. Sometimes, delaying work for clearer skies ensures the

integrity of your artistry and respects the client's investment.

If it's not raining, it might be digging conditions. You need to watch the weather and take measures, keep holes covered or work late some days before the weather moves in. Most of the time, talking to the client is a must; they might see you as wanting to avoid working in the rain. I am more than happy to work, but we will make more mess, and we will need to spend extra time clearing up. From an artist's point of view, if the weather conditions are not good and your head is down, you are not going to produce your best work, so it is better to move or wait for better weather.

Balancing the Budget
For the solopreneur, maintaining a keen eye on the budget is critical. While minor miscalculations on a small project can often be absorbed, more significant undertakings require meticulous financial planning to prevent overruns from undermining your business's stability. Embrace strategic planning, precise cost estimations, and regular budgetary reviews as your financial compasses.

Only take on prominent features with experience. Pass off the projects to your network and work on the project. It's much better for your mental health unless you are fantastic at strategic planning; precise cost estimation and regular budget reviews are crucial in mitigating such risks.

Incorporating a contingency fund within the budget and negotiating favourable terms with suppliers can provide a buffer against unforeseen expenses, ensuring the project's financial stability. Profit is the reward you get for risk. If you risk your company, you should be able to make good money. The biggest risk in life is not taking one. I am saying, "Calculate your risks". Don't go under just because you want to take on a challenge.

Flexibility, adept problem-solving capabilities, and open lines of client communication are indispensable qualities for professionals navigating the challenges of water feature projects. Adapting to unexpected changes, whether in design preferences, site conditions, or material availability, requires a proactive and innovative approach. Keeping clients informed and involved in decision-making when deviations from the initial plan are necessary helps maintain trust and manage expectations.

This collaborative approach strengthens the client-professional relationship and ensures that project adjustments are made with mutual understanding and agreement, fostering a sense of partnership in overcoming obstacles and achieving the envisioned outcome.

Mastering Flexibility and Communication

The hallmark of a seasoned water feature professional is the ability to pivot gracefully in the face of unforeseen changes and challenges. Cultivating problem-solving prowess and an open and proactive communication style fortify your ability to adjust project plans while maintaining client confidence and satisfaction. Embracing this flexible, collaborative approach cements your reputation as a reliable and adaptable professional. It enhances the overall project experience for your clients, making every water feature a testament to shared success.

For solopreneurs in the water feature industry, managing projects can seem daunting amidst the creative and physical demands of their craft. Yet, the strategic application of project management principles and the judicious use of supporting tools can transform this challenge into a streamlined, efficient process that enhances project delivery and elevates client satisfaction and business growth.

Project Management: From Conception to Completion Simplified

Managing a water feature project from conception to completion involves several critical stages, each demanding attention to detail, clear communication, and an unwavering commitment to quality.

Understanding and implementing project management fundamentals is crucial, even for solopreneurs. These principles guide you from the initial client consultation to the joyful moment of project completion.

Developing a Project Plan

Creating a detailed project plan is the foundation for all project activities. This plan encompasses every step, from the initial client inquiry to the final installation. Here's a streamlined approach tailored for solopreneurs in the water feature industry.

Initial Phone Consultation

The journey begins when a potential client reaches out. This initial interaction is crucial for pre-qualifying the prospect. Utilise this time to understand their vision, gauge their investment level, and outline what the project will and will not include. Employing software to streamline this process, with pre-filled descriptions and water feature packages, can significantly enhance efficiency. Discussing investment levels early on sets clear expectations, preventing surprises.

Design Consultation

Leverage the insights gained from the phone consultation to craft a preliminary design that captures the client's desires within the practical confines of their space. Whether using simple visual aids or more detailed artist impressions for larger projects, this step solidifies the project's scope and aesthetic direction. Upon deposit collection, further refine the design through formal drawings or digital renderings, always keeping an open channel for feedback.

Installation, Preparation and Resource Allocation

Once the design is green-lit, the focus shifts to meticulous preparation. This entails securing materials, equipment, and manpower, ensuring you're fully equipped to bring the design to life without delays. Proactive communication with suppliers and strategic planning regarding logistics are key. Remember, keeping the client engaged with updates during this phase can build anticipation and maintain excitement.

Task Scheduling and Milestone Setting

Break the project into manageable tasks, assigning realistic deadlines to each. Tools like Gantt charts can be invaluable here, visually representing the project timeline and task interdependencies. Establishing milestones—for instance, design approval, excavation start, or landscaping completion—provides clear checkpoints to evaluate progress and make necessary adjustments.

Installation Process
Begin with a thorough pre-job walkthrough, ensuring all parties share a unified vision before breaking ground. Throughout the installation, adhere to the agreed-upon design, documenting progress for client updates and future reference. Monitoring and adjusting as necessary keeps the project agile and on track.

Post-Installation Support
Project closure is more than just completing the installation. It's about ensuring the client's vision has been realised to their complete satisfaction and using the opportunity to reflect and learn. Conduct a detailed review of the work, address any lingering issues, walk the client through their new water feature, provide maintenance guidance, and answer any lingering questions. Periodic follow-ups underscore your commitment to their long-term enjoyment of the feature.

By embedding these structured yet flexible strategies into your project management approach, you streamline your workflow, elevate the quality of your installations, and satisfy your clients, laying a solid foundation for sustainable business growth.

Choosing the Right Project Management Tools and Software

As your business grows, embracing project management software becomes increasingly beneficial. While the thought of migrating from a flexible, spontaneous approach to a more structured system may seem intimidating, user-friendly tools like Trello, Asana, QuickBooks, Xero, Slack, Microsoft Teams, AutoCAD, or SketchUp can revolutionise how you organise and execute projects. These platforms allow for efficient task organisation, budget tracking, team communication, and detailed project visualisation, thereby freeing you to concentrate on delivering exceptional quality and maintaining strong client relationships.

For solopreneurs, the key lies in selecting software that aligns with your needs while minimising complexity. Start with simple and flexible tools, allowing you to maintain the personal touch that distinguishes your brand. Whether keeping an inventory of materials, managing your schedule, or communicating with clients, the right technology can make these tasks less time-consuming, letting you focus on what you do best—creating beautiful water features.

Embracing these strategies and tools, you can streamline your operations, ensure quality control, and foster client communication and satisfaction, laying a solid foundation for your business's future growth. Whether you remain a solo operator or expand your team, these project management practices will remain a cornerstone of your success, enabling you to deliver projects that delight your clients and distinguish your work.

Navigating Growth and Collaboration

Despite often working alone, you may occasionally collaborate with others for more extensive installations. Clear communication and a protective oversight of your time are essential to ensure seamless project integration.

As you contemplate the journey of growth and expansion within the water feature industry, it's essential to recognise the pivotal moments when scaling your operations or collaborating with others, which might transform from a general idea into a tangible strategy for advancement. This chapter's concluding section seeks to illuminate the path toward judiciously expanding your solo endeavour or forging partnerships with fellow solopreneurs, offering a blueprint for growth that respects the essence of your craft while opening doors to new possibilities.

Strategic Delegation and Outsourcing

The evolution of your water feature business may lead to opportunities where delegation or outsourcing becomes not just beneficial but necessary for continued growth and sustainability. Identifying tasks that lie beyond your core competencies or consume disproportionate amounts of your time, such as detailed financial management, digital marketing efforts, or even specific technical aspects of projects, and entrusting them to skilled professionals can significantly enhance your operational efficiency.

This strategic approach allows you to remain focused on what you enjoy: the creative and technical execution of water features. It ensures that each project continues to embody the quality and innovation that define your work. Choosing collaborators who align with your values and quality standards is crucial, as their contributions will directly reflect on your brand and the satisfaction of your clients.

Collaboration and Team Dynamics

As projects increase in scale or complexity, the prospect of coordinating with a team, whether comprised of employees, subcontractors, or partners from within your network of solopreneurs, becomes an integral aspect of project management. Here are foundational strategies to foster effective team dynamics:

- **Clear communication**
  Establishing and maintaining open communication channels ensures that everyone involved is aligned with project goals, timelines, and expectations, facilitating a cohesive effort toward shared objectives.
- **Defined roles and responsibilities**
  Clarifying each team member's specific roles and contributions helps eliminate confusion and overlap, ensuring a streamlined approach to project execution.
- **Proactive conflict resolution**
  Adopting a proactive stance toward resolving disagreements or challenges promotes a harmonious work environment and maintains project momentum.
- **Encouraging collaboration**
  Cultivating a culture that values each team member's input and expertise enriches the project outcome and fosters a sense of shared achievement and pride in the work accomplished.

Envisioning the Future

Considering growth and expansion as part of your business's evolution invites a shift in perspective, viewing each project as a standalone endeavour and a stepping stone toward broader horizons. Whether this means scaling your solo operation, forming alliances with other solopreneurs for collaborative ventures, or transitioning to a model incorporating a more extensive team dynamic, each step forward is an opportunity to refine your approach, expand your impact, and continue delivering water features that enchant and inspire. This strategic vision for growth, grounded in the principles and practices outlined throughout this chapter, prepares you to confidently navigate the future, ready to embrace new challenges and opportunities in the ever-evolving landscape of the water feature industry.

Part 4:
MAXIMISING PROFIT AND IMPACT

"The more money you make, the bigger impact (POND) you can create."
- John G

9
FINANCIAL STRATEGIES

Running a successful water feature business involves much more than artistic skill and technical know-how—it demands a solid grasp of your numbers. This chapter is designed to transform how you approach your business' financial aspects, from pricing and cost management to strategic financial planning. By simplifying complex financial concepts and breaking the content into clear, manageable sections, this guide aims to empower you with the tools needed for financial success.

Key Sections:

- **Managing costs effectively**
  Dive into the various cost components of pond projects, such as materials, labour, and overhead.
- **Discover practical strategies for keeping costs under control and enhancing project profitability**

- **Pricing your services for profit**
  Learn to craft a pricing strategy that captures the actual value of your services. Understand how to calculate costs, set competitive markups, and justify premium prices to clients.
- **Diversifying revenue streams**
  Explore expanding your income sources through additional services and product sales. Consider package pricing and offering maintenance plans.

The water feature industry is a niche sector that offers significant financial opportunities and requires effective strategic planning. Understanding the following trends is essential to planning and strategising effectively, as they directly influence customer preferences, pricing strategies, and the types of services in demand. There is an increasing trend among consumers to opt for eco-friendly and sustainable water features.

This shift has led to new market segments and premium pricing for low-maintenance solutions. Innovations like automated dosing systems and energy-efficient pumps shape customer expectations and project specifications. Early adoption of these technologies can be a significant differentiator. There has been a surge in homeowners' interest in improving their outdoor living spaces, increasing the demand for custom but packaged water features.

Managing Costs Effectively

It's crucial to understand all project costs, including direct costs like materials and labour and indirect costs such as overhead. Pricing your water features and services for profit requires deeply understanding of your costs, market dynamics, and client expectations. By adopting a structured approach to package pricing, accurately calculating labour costs, employing effective sales techniques, and committing to continuous analysis, you can establish a pricing strategy that promotes profitability and sustainability in the competitive landscape of water feature and water feature construction.

Direct Costs
Labour
This includes your time; if you are an owner-operator, as a true solopreneur, you need to be paid twice, so then, when you replace yourself in the hole, you still get paid for running the business (some will include this in the overhead, don't forget it). This cost is vital; you need skilled labour for almost every part of the project: marketing and sales, planning and design work, installation (not all skilled, but are you doing

everything?), and possibly maintenance services post-installation.

Your labour costs can fluctuate based on the project's location, the need to travel to pick up materials, and the level of expertise required. Moving stuff around is part of the job but not the whole job. Managers are needed if unskilled labour is on-site; however, you do only need one person on site who is in charge.

Materials

These costs after labour are often the most significant and can include everything from pumps and liners to rocks and plants. The cost of materials can vary widely depending on the complexity and size of the project.

Indirect Costs

Overhead

Overhead expenses encompass indirect costs such as stuff that still has to get paid even if you stay in bed or don't produce anything that day. These costs could include training, equipment costs and maintenance, rentals and utilities, company brand marketing, attending trade shows, and all admin duties like sending and receiving emails. These costs don't directly contribute to a single project but are necessary for running the business.

Unforeseen Expenses
Unexpected costs arise during a project, such as additional materials needed due to miscalculations or extended labour hours from unforeseen technical challenges or untrained staff. On-site training does happen, and you still have to pay people for training. Increase your labour hours if people are learning on-site or when someone is doing marketing on the job site and the job producing money.

Include a contingency budget within your project estimates to cover unforeseen expenses. Depending on the complexity, I would mark up at least 10-20% of the total project cost after working everything out. You're better off this way around. If you don't need it, you can put that money to a good cause.

Efficient Material Management
Establish strong relationships with suppliers to secure better prices and ensure the availability of high-quality materials. Consider bulk purchases or early buys for common materials to reduce costs.

Skilled Labour Utilisation
"Who", not "how", is sometimes called for. Find your "whos" (which people can do this job) and ask yourself, can I pay someone to do this task? Is this a ten-pound-an-hour job? Ensure high efficiency and reduce the

likelihood of costly mistakes. Utilising skilled labour effectively also means planning the workforce according to project demands to avoid under or overstaffing. It's a fine line as a solopreneur: Bring in help as needed, but don't put yourself out of work. Focus on what you want to do and reduce the other stuff.

Control Overhead Costs
Regularly review and optimise overhead expenses, such as using software and automation to streamline administrative tasks.

The True Costs of Doing Business

When I started understanding the actual costs, my business changed. In 2012, I started Any Pond Limited after working for myself for nine years. This marked the beginning of owning an actual business. At first, it was just me with occasional help, but in 2014, we expanded by hiring a full-time staff member. This expansion was a turning point, forcing Any Pond Limited over the VAT threshold. Within that year, I doubled the company's revenue through strategic financial management and broadening our service offerings. Instead of doing 80-100 hour weeks, I would work three or four days in the hole overseeing my help, and on Friday, I would force myself to do the office work and financials.

We introduced package pricing and pre-paid seasonal maintenance plans, which provided an income stream during the typically slower months from September to March. This income secured our overhead and gave us time in people's gardens, another touchpoint, a chance to show and inspire upsells like our bacteria products and other services.

Adopting a transparent pricing model was crucial; it fostered trust and helped retain customers. I provided pre-written detailed quotations that broke down the line items and benefits, enabling clients to appreciate the value of the initial installation and the ongoing maintenance services. Utilising tools like FreshBooks, custom budgeting tools, and my hourly rate calculator, we meticulously tracked data on the job site, expenses and profits. This precise financial oversight was vital for swiftly adjusting business strategies to stay efficient and profitable. Understanding why projects ran over or needed to charge more was crucial for the success.

At the same time, I spoke about the costs online and in blogs, and I recorded videos about our value-based pricing, which significantly bolstered our market position. I invested a lot in professional DSLR photography and video production equipment (now you only need your phone), enhancing the presentation of our projects across social media and our website.

My focus then turned to helping people Dream, Plan, and Enjoy ponds and water features while justifying our premium pricing based on aquatic art and environmental value rather than simply competing on cost. Often, our rates were double or even triple those of competitors, yet this approach attracted a discerning clientele who valued unique and sustainable solutions.

Our strong online presence, notably through humorous content to attract attention and increase engagement on Facebook, backed up by in-depth instructional YouTube videos, helped distinguish Any Pond Limited as a trusted resource in the UK for ponds and water features.

Pricing Your Services for Profit

Once all your costs are calculated, setting a markup that ensures profitability is critical. Your business can establish pricing models that ensure profitability and align with exceptional value. This approach fosters a transparent and trusting relationship with clients, enhancing customer satisfaction and business sustainability.

You must pay your bills daily to keep the business alive. The goal of any game or business is to keep you playing; if you are not enjoying the game or business, change it.

Packing up the old business or game might take some effort, but you need to do this to start the new game. Try to play only one game at a time. You can't sit on two toilets; focus on one and be a master of it.

Successful pricing in the water feature industry requires a blend of strategic thinking and a deep understanding of the value offered through craftsmanship and customisation. This section explores effective pricing strategies, emphasising how to set prices that cover costs, ensure a profit, and accurately reflect the quality and uniqueness of the services provided.

Cost Calculation
Sum up all the direct costs associated with a project. Remember to factor in costs such as travelling expenses and transport. Are you hand-picking rocks? Do you need any special tools or equipment?

Setting Markups
Sum up all the indirect costs and divide this by the days you work in the hole (remember rainy days, I base mine on a three-day work week). Ask yourself all the time: Who is paying for this? A common practice is to apply a markup percentage to your costs to cover overhead and your desired profit margin.

Due to the specialised skills and unique design elements, a higher markup can often be justified for custom aquatic art and other high-ticket projects. A typical markup should be 50 to 80%, depending on the complexity and customisation level.

Only some things need to be marked up (many ways to price work). If you aim to sell hours, materials don't all need to be marked up 50% (but let's avoid getting into that here that comes with more people in the hole). When starting to look at your numbers, it's best to cover everything until you understand your overhead like a ninja. Always make sure your overhead is being covered; if your backpack is too big, look at reducing things in it or hiring more people to carry the indirect costs (this extra production comes with the need to sell more. However, you might be able to drop prices when you bring on more people).

Importance of Transparency

Transparency in pricing builds trust with clients and can help prequalify leads, saving time and focusing efforts on serious inquiries.

Menu Pricing
Develop transparent, straightforward pricing for different water features and related services. Display this

on your website's pricing tab. If you produce hard marketing materials, remember I prefer using QR codes. Then, you can change your prices without having to reprint. This transparency and options allow potential clients to understand what they can expect to pay before they need to talk to someone.

I still prefer QR codes for special offers during the shows as they allow you to hand out material, which can then be kept. One lady kept my postcard for seven years before being able to afford a new garden pond. During the garden shows, showgoers would need to scan the QR code for pricing instead of looking at a price tag and needing help understanding it. Also, it gives you or your PR staff a chance to engage a little bit human-to-human.

Justifying Premium Prices

When your services are priced higher due to superior craftsmanship or outcomes, it's essential to communicate the reasons behind these prices. Detail the above and beyond service, quality or size of materials, the bespoke custom design process, and the level of training needed to produce this. Remember the long-term value and enjoyment of a well-executed water feature. You understand or should understand what affects the feature's price, so it's your job to educate your potential customers so they can shop or pick what they want.

Competitive Pricing Models

Creating competitive pricing models requires understanding both the market and the unique value you offer.

Market Research

First, don't just copy the market pricing. Know your numbers and use this against the data first and foremost. Of course, understand the pricing landscape by researching competitors (note they might not be making money or can charge less than you due to their business model). What are others charging for similar services (do you see any gaps)? How do your services differ (skill set, location, clientele, you give a seven-star personalised service)?

Client Value Reflection

Your pricing model should reflect the value perceived by the client. Consider factors like the longevity, functionality, aesthetic appeal, and maintenance requirements of the features you install.

Value-Based Pricing

Value-based pricing focuses on the perceived worth of your service to the customer rather than just the cost to produce it. This approach can significantly enhance profitability if implemented correctly:

- **Understanding client perception**
  Engage with clients to understand what aspects of your service they value most. Is it the bespoke design, the quality of materials, the brand reputation, or the overall reliability and professionalism?
- **Communicating value**
  Use testimonials, case studies, and past work portfolios to demonstrate the quality and value of your services. Make sure to highlight how your water features enhance property value, provide a tranquil retreat, or serve as a focal point for family gatherings.
- **Pricing strategy**
  Set prices that align with the value delivered. For example, suppose your designs are unique or use exceptionally high-quality or sustainable materials. In that case, these should be priced accordingly to reflect their cost and the added value they provide to the client.

Diversifying Revenue Streams

By diversifying your revenue streams, you cushion the business against fluctuations in demand and enhance your service offerings, making your business a one-stop shop for all water feature needs. This approach increases marketability and strengthens your financial stability, helping you grow a robust, resilient business. Adding complementary services enhances customer value and can lead to increased customer retention and higher revenue per project.

Options to Consider

Maintenance Plans

Develop comprehensive maintenance plans that include regular check-ups and service calls. If you handle ongoing maintenance, consider offering packages with automatic dosing systems or extended warranties.

Fish and Plants

You can harvest fish and plants from your client's ponds and gardens. This is a service to the pond owner, as you are splitting, dividing, and rehoming unwanted fish. Charge both clients for these services as time and bio-security measures must be considered.

Water Feature Enhancements

Offer services to upgrade existing features, such as integrating modern technology, improving water quality systems, or making aesthetic enhancements.

Water Feature Upgrades

Provide services to enhance or repair existing installations, such as adding nighttime illumination packages, water treatment solutions, or updating filtration systems and the landscaping elements surrounding the feature.

Extra Soft or Hard Landscaping

Extend your offerings to include rockeries to match your stonework, edging borders with rock, creating a mountainscape (like recreating a natural setting on a miniature scale), and planting around the water features. This holistic approach can appeal to clients seeking a complete hands-free service.

Consulting Services

Offer your expertise to other businesses or individuals looking to design water features. This can be done through one-on-one consulting or group workshops. These other businesses might be building the whole garden, and you can be in charge of helping with the water feature,

Public Speaking

Engage with the community online (Facebook groups) and offline by offering talks at gardening clubs, schools, or local events. This raises your profile and can lead to direct business inquiries and partnerships.

Referral Programs

Offer referral fees or packages to businesses or individuals sharing your product or service idea. If they design gardens, build houses, or get in front of your ideal clients, offer them packages.

Seasonal Product Bundles

Assemble and sell curated packages of water feature care supplies, similar to seasonal baskets or hampers. The packages can include treatments, fish food, cleaning tools, and decorative items.

Strategic Partnerships

Partner with suppliers, local garden centres, or other relevant businesses. These partnerships can offer mutual benefits, such as shared marketing efforts or exclusive deals on supplies.

Retail Sales

Consider selling water feature-related products directly to your customers online. Be that one-stop shop. This could include pumps, liners, water plants, fish stock, or decorative elements. Of course, this will lead to more installation and servicing work.

Financial Planning and Management

Effective budgeting and financial forecasting are crucial, even for a solopreneur. As your business approaches or exceeds revenue milestones, such as the £100K mark, financial planning becomes increasingly important to sustain growth and manage resources efficiently.

Simplifying Financial Planning
Small businesses can use financial tools to automate much of the budgeting and forecasting process. Software like QuickBooks or Xero can help you visualise your financial health, track expenses, and predict future cash flows more accurately.

Project-Based Budgeting
Create budgets for each project, considering all potential costs, from materials to subcontractor fees. This approach helps ensure that each project is profitable and you're not underquoting your services.

Regular Financial Reviews
Set a weekly, monthly, or quarterly routine to review your financial projections versus actual income and expenses. This will help you adjust your business strategies quickly, ensuring you remain on target to meet your financial goals.

Managing Cash Flow

For a solopreneur, managing cash flow effectively is straightforward but crucial to avoiding financial strain as your business grows and begins to carry stock or handle larger projects.

Efficient Invoicing Practices

Implement invoicing systems that allow you to bill clients promptly. Use mobile invoicing apps to send invoices immediately upon closing the deal, completing a job or reaching a project milestone.

Advance Payments and Deposits

Secure payments upfront or stagger payments at various project stages. This improves cash flow and provides funds for project expenses before they occur.

Avoid Working Past Payment Deadlines

Establish clear payment terms with your clients and stick to them. If a project payment is delayed, halt further work until payment is made. This practice ensures that you only extend credit with intention and keeps your business's financial health stable.

Expense Tracking

Keep meticulous records of all fixed and variable expenses. Use apps or software that sync with your bank accounts and categorise expenses automatically, helping you keep a real-time pulse on where your money goes.

Financial Cushion

Aim to maintain a reserve fund, or financial cushion, that covers at least three to six months of operational expenses. This fund can be a lifesaver during the winter or if unexpected expenses arise.

Leveraging Financial Tools and Resources

Having robust financial tools can streamline numerous accounting tasks, from project costing to financial reporting, making these processes less time-consuming and more accurate.

For a long time, FreshBooks was my favourite accounting software. This tool is particularly suited for solopreneur water feature professionals. I didn't use all the functions but played around with the time tracking and project management features. My accountants could use the information but preferred other software.

FreshBooks made invoicing and following up on late payments straightforward, helping me maintain a healthy cash flow. I loved how quick it was with the mobile app. Estimating in the garden with pre-loaded line items and knowing if clients had opened up the files was a game changer. Sometimes, I would have to reword the items, but I loved that it was mobile-friendly.

We have now moved on to **Xero** for all our accounting software. I love its financial reporting features; our bookkeeper is a wiz at using it. Like FreshBooks, it is cloud-based, and Xero is the next choice if you have office-based help or staff someone other than you. It facilitates real-time financial monitoring and collaboration with our accountants so they can pull up stuff on Zoom meetings, ensuring we always have a clear view of our business' financial health.

QuickBooks

Another market leader for many other professionals across the big pond. I started on a version supplied via my bank then, but this needed to be mobile-friendly. I hear it's got better, and some people love it. QuickBooks is an idea for project costing, invoicing, and financial tracking. It offers a variety of integrations with other tools and platforms, which can automate almost all aspects of your financial management.

Professional Financial Advice

While financial software can handle much of the day-to-day accounting and financial management, there are times when professional advice is invaluable, particularly in areas like tax planning and business structuring.

Tax Planning

A qualified accountant can help you structure your business to maximise tax efficiencies, ensure you're paying only what you need, and advise you on applicable tax credits or deductions.

Business Structuring

As your business grows, a financial advisor can suggest the most appropriate business structure (sole proprietorship, partnership, limited company, etc) to optimise tax and legal benefits. This structure can influence everything from your liability in the business to how you can take profits out.

Investment Strategies

Financial advisors provide crucial advice on risk management and portfolio diversification if you want to invest profits back into the business or even into external opportunities.

Incorporating These Tools and Resources

Integrating sophisticated accounting software and consulting with financial experts ensures that your financial practices support robust business growth and development. These tools not only help in managing day-to-day financial operations but also in planning long-term strategies that secure your business's future. This approach allows you to focus on what you do best—

designing and installing beautiful water features—while maintaining peace of mind that your financial bases are covered.

What is the Next Step in Financials?

While working for yourself, the next step is creating a business you can sell. When examining the financials of your single-person water feature business, you should focus on more than just the immediate profits. It would be best to consider how to shape your business venture into an asset that can be sold.

What will buyers want? If you were buying a business, what would you see value in?

>   Customer database
>   Great website with lead gen
>   Well-respected company brand
>   Scalable services
>   Documented processes
>   Ahead in technology and trends

10

EXPANDING YOUR BUSINESS

Welcome to the most crucial chapter. If you want to grow your business, you've come to the right place. But be warned: This chapter requires an open mindset and a willingness to change. It's like in the movie The Matrix—you can take the truth pill, which will awaken you to the real world. But this journey calls for a leap of faith. You'll need to let go of the handrail or jump, and there's no turning back once you do…

To get started, find a comfortable spot away from distractions and unplug if necessary. Scaling your business is an exciting prospect but comes with challenges and opportunities. Striking the right balance is crucial, as well as knowing when to push forward and when to consolidate your gains. It's important to understand that true freedom in business comes from discipline and structured growth. You'll need to shift your mindset and approach to move from working in your business to working on your business.

Throughout this chapter, I'll provide practical guidance and comprehensive content to help you scale your business effectively. Whether you continue this journey is up to you, but my goal is to prepare you to transition from a solopreneur to a leader of a thriving enterprise.

I might not know you by name, but I know you have a dream!

The Fear of Letting Go

For years, I prided myself on the quality and personal touch I brought to each pond installation. The thought of not being physically present at job sites filled me with anxiety. What if the quality suffered? What if my team needed me and I wasn't there? These questions haunted me as I considered expanding my operations.

The transition began when I forced myself to step back. At first, I constantly wanted to be called out to the sites. I wanted to be needed, to jump in and solve problems. But gradually, I realised that my constant presence could be unsustainable and unnecessary for the success of the projects. I found myself thinking about parents dropping kids off at school. I don't have kids, but I had staff that could do a lot of damage with my neck on the line.

Moment of Realisation

I distinctly remember a day when the team encountered a significant issue with seaming a liner. My immediate instinct was to rush to the site. However, I paused and asked, "Do you need me to come out, or can you handle it?" The team hesitated but then confidently said they could manage. That day, they resolved the issue and gained a valuable boost in their problem-solving confidence. This was a turning point for me. Could I trust them? Yes. Could I hand off everything? No, my job was to help with some sales and marketing. I was handing my guys leads, and that turned into sales. Now, I am empowered to let the sales staff be more daring and dynamic, with some guidelines in place.

Building a reliable team meant establishing systems that did not require my constant oversight. I began to focus more on training and developing clear guidelines and processes. This shift allowed me to manage the business without being overwhelmed by day-to-day operational challenges, even to the point of asking the team to develop systems when ones were not put into place.

Every missed deadline or hiccup on the job became a learning experience, not just for the team but also for me. I learned to trust their judgement and to provide guidance without taking over. Yes, I could build ponds quicker and better, but that wasn't the point. It was about building a team that could operate with the same passion and precision without my direct hand.

Embracing the Role of a Leader

The hardest part was redefining my role from a doer to a leader. I had to accept that my value to the business was crafting and leading a company that crafts water features. This meant less time in the hole and more time in the office strategising, marketing, and expanding the business footprint.

An actual test came when I planned a four-week business trip abroad and then a further four days of travelling with a vendor before hosting customers for a garden party—a daunting thought for someone who never wanted to step away. To my surprise, not only did the business operate smoothly in my absence, but it also thrived and made money. It was great turning up at our company garden party after guests arrived. This real breakaway proved to the team and me that the systems were robust and the business I built was sustainable beyond my physical presence.

These experiences taught me that letting go doesn't mean losing control. It means empowering others and stepping into a role that ensures the business's growth and longevity. It was about understanding that discipline and structure lead to freedom—freedom from daily operations and freedom to focus on scaling and enriching the business.

This personal and professional transformation journey has been filled with moments of fear, growth, and ultimate satisfaction. It's a testament that a solopreneur can evolve into a successful business owner, guiding a team towards shared success without micromanaging every detail.

Are You Ready for Growth?

If you're considering expanding your business, you must ask yourself some tough questions to determine whether you're ready to take the next step. Only you can answer these questions. Expanding requires carefully assessing your current business structure, market conditions, and your preparedness to handle growth.

Why did you start this business?

Understanding the difference between creating a job for yourself and building a self-sustaining business is crucial. You may have created a job for yourself if you are involved in every detail and cannot step away daily for a few weeks or even months. Therefore, it is essential to ask yourself whether your efforts are worth the rewards you are receiving. This section will guide you from being self-employed to becoming a business owner. As a business owner, your role will shift towards overseeing operations instead of managing every task.

Scaling your business comes with its own set of challenges. Maintaining the quality of work, the culture of your company, and the level of customer service can become increasingly difficult as you expand. This chapter provides practical advice on managing these critical aspects effectively. From implementing systems that ensure quality control to developing a team that shares your vision and values, I cover essential strategies to help you grow without compromising the core aspects of your business that made you successful in the first place.

Here are some essential things to consider:
- Are your processes efficient and streamlined?
- Do you have the right talent to support growth?
- Is the market favourable for expansion?

Understanding these elements will help you decide whether now is the right time to scale your business.

In each section, you'll gain valuable insights and actionable strategies to help you achieve manageable, sustainable growth aligned with your long-term goals. Prepare to transform your operations and mindset as you expand your business in the dynamic world of water features.

Conduct a Comprehensive Business Audit

It is crucial to thoroughly evaluate your garden water feature business before expanding it. This evaluation will help you identify your strengths, weaknesses, and areas needing improvement to handle growth successfully. Whether you are a new business owner or have been operating for several years, assessing your progress is essential. If this is your first time doing this, don't worry. These steps are necessary for growth. As the saying goes, "Big oak trees grow mighty from small acorns."

I highly recommend conducting this exercise. I did a version of this audit for the first time while on an aeroplane on my way to my first proper business trip. It was a powerful experience, and I couldn't turn back even if I wanted to. Look down and visualise your business from a bird's eye view or drone to see a bigger picture.

I put myself into aeroplane mode mentally almost every day now. I am doing it right now, writing this book.

So, let's get started and look closely at your business.

Operational Efficiency
Start by assessing the efficiency of your current operations. Are your processes streamlined enough to handle increased demand? Examine your project management systems, supplier relationships, and technology use. Identifying and addressing operational bottlenecks now is vital as they can hinder expansion.

Financial Health
A healthy financial status is critical for expansion. Review your business's financial statements, including profit margins, cash flow, debt levels, and revenue growth trends. Understanding your financial capacity will help you determine how much you can invest in growth without overextending.

Market Position
Analyse your position within the industry. Are you a leading player in your local area or a smaller entity looking to grow? Understanding your market share and the competitive landscape helps you strategise for expansion. Consider conducting market research to

identify trends and customer needs that are currently unmet.

Customer Satisfaction

Customer loyalty is a cornerstone of any expanding business. Gauge customer satisfaction through feedback, reviews, and repeat business rates. High satisfaction indicates your company is ready to expand, as happy customers will likely continue supporting and promoting your brand.

Now that your audit is complete, you can look ahead to where you want to be. To do this successfully, you must keep your vision clear and your goals focused. Expansion requires precise planning goals to structure your growth effectively.

Set **S**pecific, **M**easurable, **A**chievable, **R**elevant, and **T**ime-bound (SMART) goals that align with your business's capacity and market opportunities. For instance, a SMART goal might be to increase your fountain customer base by 25% within the next year through new digital marketing strategies around your fountain installations.

A clear vision of what your business will look like post-expansion is also essential.

Envision your future business state; fast forward a year or three:

- What new services or products will you offer?
- What's the new size of your catchment area?
- How many more customers do you need for a new employee?

Establish realistic milestones for reaching this vision, such as launching a new maintenance program in the next six months or entering two new counties in the next year.

By thoroughly assessing your business's readiness for expansion and setting clear, actionable goals, you can ensure that your growth will be sustainable and aligned with your long-term business objectives. This foundational work is crucial for building a resilient business that grows and thrives in its expanded form.

Strategies for Scaling Operations

As you prepare to expand your water feature business, optimising operational efficiency and broadening your service offerings are key strategies. This section provides practical advice on integrating technology to streamline operations and explores new market opportunities to diversify your services.

Process Automation and Technology Adoption

Integrating technology to automate business processes is crucial to handle increased demand effectively. Automation can streamline workflows, reduce human error, and free up your time to focus on more strategic tasks. For instance, Customer Relationship Management (CRM) software can automate customer interactions, follow-ups, and service scheduling, ensuring nothing slips through the cracks as your business grows.

Recent industry studies have shown that automation significantly enhances operational efficiency. Moreover, businesses that implement automation in customer communications and project management report a reduced time spent on administrative tasks by up to 30%. Such efficiency improvements can lead to better customer service and increased capacity to handle more projects.

For example, menu pricing can significantly simplify the estimating time for standard services. By implementing this approach, sales staff can assist customers in selecting options more efficiently, which enhances the overall customer shopping experience. In addition, using digital estimation tools that automatically update pricing can save time on manual calculations.

Another way to streamline operations is to develop customer self-service portals where customers can directly select and customise services, reducing the workload on sales staff and empowering customers to make their own choices.

Technology also greatly assists people who experience problems with traditional communication methods, such as dyslexia and other challenges (like myself). Several useful tools are available, including transcription and read-back software that can convert speech to text and text to speech, making communication more straightforward and professional. Also, grammar and writing assistants, such as Grammarly, can help refine emails and proposals, ensuring that they adhere to professional standards without requiring significant time to invest.

Market Demand and Service Feasibility
Thorough market research must assess demand and feasibility before adding new services. Analyse customer needs, market trends, and competitor offerings to identify gaps your business could fill. Consider new services' logistical and financial implications to ensure they can be delivered effectively and profitably.

By adopting strategic approaches to operational efficiency and service expansion, you can ensure that your business grows in scale, capability, and profitability.

Building and Managing a Competent Team

Developing a skilled and cohesive team becomes essential as your water feature business grows. This part focuses on effective hiring strategies and team development to ensure a capable and harmonious workforce supports your expanding business.

Hiring Strategies for Scaling

- **Recruitment and culture fit**

  Finding the right team members starts with understanding the specific skills your business needs. Create detailed job descriptions that list required skills and communicate your company culture and the attributes that align with it. Effective recruitment strategies involve screening for competence and cultural fit, ensuring new hires share your business values and vision. Utilising platforms like LinkedIn and job boards can help attract candidates who are already tuned into the sector's demands and culture.

- **Structured onboarding**

  Once suitable candidates are hired, a structured onboarding process is crucial to successfully integrating them into your team. This should include comprehensive training on your business processes, in-depth introductions to all team members, and clear communication of job roles and expectations.

A well-defined onboarding process accelerates new hires' productivity and enhances their engagement and commitment to the company's goals.

Team Development and Leadership

- **Training and team-building**

    Continuous professional development is vital to maintaining a skilled team supporting business growth. Implement regular training programs that enhance technical skills in water feature design and installation and soft skills such as customer service and project management. Team-building activities can strengthen relationships among team members, fostering a collaborative environment that supports effective problem-solving and innovation.

- **Leadership development**

    As your business expands, so does the need for strong leadership. Leadership development programs are vital for preparing yourself and potential managers within your team to lead effectively, primarily through periods of significant change. Focus on developing skills such as strategic decision-making, conflict resolution, and motivational techniques that ensure leaders can guide their teams efficiently and maintain morale during growth phases.

By investing in comprehensive hiring strategies and continuous team development, you can build a workforce that meets your business's current needs and is prepared to handle future challenges and opportunities. This approach ensures that your team remains a strong pillar of support as your business evolves, driving sustained growth and success in the competitive water feature industry.

Forging Beneficial Partnerships

Expanding your water feature business often requires more than internal growth; it can also benefit significantly from strategic partnerships. This section guides you through identifying potential partners and managing these relationships effectively to support your business's expansion and market reach.

Identifying Potential Partners

- **Alignment with growth goals**

  To identify the right partners, focus on how potential collaborations can align with and support your business's growth objectives. Look for partners that can help optimise your supply chain, expand your market reach, or enhance your service offerings. For example, partnering with a supplier could ensure better material rates or more reliable material availability. At the same time, a partnership with a design firm could help you tap into new customer segments.

- **Due diligence**
  Conducting thorough due diligence is critical to ensuring that potential partners are financially sound, share your business values, and have a reliable track record. Investigate their business practices and market reputation and review any previous partnership outcomes. This process helps mitigate risks and lays the foundation for a partnership based on trust and mutual respect.

Negotiating and Managing Partnerships
- **Creating mutually beneficial agreements**
  When negotiating partnership agreements, aim for terms that foster long-term collaboration. This involves understanding and addressing the strategic goals of both parties. Ensure the agreements include clear profit-sharing terms, responsibilities, and conflict resolution mechanisms. Legal consultation can help safeguard your interests and ensure the partnership agreement is balanced and transparent.

- **Partnership management**
  Effective partnership management is crucial for maintaining healthy and productive relationships.

Establish regular communication channels to ensure all parties are aligned, and any issues are addressed promptly. Regular meetings, performance reviews, and updates on business developments help maintain the partnership's vitality and relevance. Clear expectations and shared goals are also essential, keeping both parties focused on the partnership's objectives.

By carefully selecting the right partners, negotiating equitable agreements, and diligently managing these relationships, you can leverage external expertise and resources to scale your business more effectively. Strategic partnerships extend your operational capabilities and enhance your competitive edge in the expanding market of water features.

Overcoming Challenges in Business Expansion

As you look to expand your water feature business, several challenges may hinder your growth. This section discusses strategies to navigate these challenges, ensuring your business grows and maintains its core values and quality.

Securing Funding and Managing Cash Flow

Expanding your business often requires additional capital. Explore various funding options such as small business loans, investor funding, or reinvesting profits back into the business. Maintaining a detailed cash flow forecast is crucial to manage this new capital effectively. This helps in anticipating and covering financial gaps before they become problematic.

Resource Allocation

Efficient resource use is vital for successful expansion. Prioritise investments that offer the most significant potential returns. Monitoring how resources are deployed helps adjust strategies that do not yield expected outcomes, ensuring that every pound spent contributes to business growth.

Quality Standards and Customer Service

Rapid growth should maintain the quality of your work and the satisfaction of your customers. Maintain high standards by implementing Standard Operating Procedures (SOPs) that ensure consistency across all projects. Regular quality checks and customer feedback should be integral to your expansion strategy, allowing you to adjust practices that may not meet your traditional quality standards.

Setting the Stage for Long-Term Success

As you contemplate expanding your water feature business, remember that growth should be approached thoughtfully and strategically. Focus on long-term objectives and the overall health of your business. Expansion is not just about increasing size but about enhancing the quality of your service, the satisfaction of your customers, and the efficiency of your operations. Every challenge you face in expanding your business is an opportunity to learn and improve. Whether navigating financial hurdles, optimising resources, or managing a larger team, each obstacle gives you a chance to strengthen your business acumen.

Continuously plan and forecast your business's future. This foresight will allow you to anticipate changes in the market, adapt your strategies, and maintain a competitive edge. Regularly revisit and revise your business plans to align with current realities and prospects. As your business grows, maintain the high standards of quality and customer service that set you apart from the competition. Your commitment to excellence will continue to drive referrals, repeat business, and, ultimately, the sustainable success of your business.

Growth is a journey that requires patience, persistence, and hard work. But with the right approach, it can also be gratifying. Remember, the ultimate success of your expansion efforts will depend on your ability to adapt, learn, and remain committed to your core values and objectives. Let this chapter be the springboard for your strategic growth and long-term success in the vibrant world of water features.

"Success is not final, failure is not fatal: It is the courage to continue that counts."
- Winston Churchill

Part 5:
BUILDING A LEGACY

"The best way to predict the future is to create it."
- Peter Drucker

11

THE FUTURE OF YOUR POND BUSINESS

The pond industry is on the cusp of significant transformations with emerging trends and potential innovations that promise to redefine traditional approaches. There is a clear need for aquatic artists who can create serene and biodiverse water features that symbolise sustainable beauty. This endeavour requires a commitment to lifelong learning, an open-minded approach to collaboration, and a willingness to explore uncharted waters of creativity.

Many contractors believe doing more work will help them reach their goals, which usually leads to creating more work for themselves. Therefore, in later years, it is crucial to consider less physically demanding roles and focus on leadership, innovation or streamlined operations that a single individual can manage effectively as we age. In this chapter, I will help you explore how each professional can contribute to a vibrant, future-oriented pond industry and inspire you to set concrete goals and make impactful decisions.

One essential aspect of future-proofing a business is remaining agile and responsive to market changes. Continuously assessing the market and adjusting business offerings to stay competitive is crucial. In this context, discussing the importance of adapting to market shifts and providing strategies can benefit businesses.

Innovations and Trends on the Horizon

This section explores the latest developments and offers insights into how entrepreneurs can use them to grow their businesses and differentiate themselves.

Standalone Rentable Features
One exciting trend gaining traction is the concept of standalone rentable water features. These portable installations are designed for temporary setups, making them perfect for events, weddings, or seasonal displays.

Here's how our businesses can capitalise on this emerging model:

Event Partnerships
Forge partners with event planners and venues to offer your rentable water features as part of their event packages.

Customisation Options
Provide customisation options for clients, allowing them to choose designs that match the theme or style of their event.

Marketing Strategy
Develop targeted marketing strategies highlighting the unique appeal and convenience of rentable water features, focusing on their aesthetic value and ease of installation.

How to Use AI to Design and Build A Water Feature

AI is set to revolutionise the garden water feature industry, but don't worry. AI will not take over or replace your job but will help you by enhancing precision, efficiency, and personalisation in design and construction.

AI can generate multiple design simulations, analyse customer preferences, and, I am guessing, assist in precisely constructing water features.

To integrate AI into your business, invest in AI tools, train your team, and showcase innovations. The future of the pond and water feature industry could see significant technological advancements, such as AI-driven design tools, automated maintenance systems, intelligent water management systems, and better VR and AR; these technologies could become more commonplace in client demonstrations, allowing them to see and interact with a virtual model of their proposed water feature in real-time and in their own space. Internet of Things (IoT) devices could be used increasingly to integrate various aspects of pond or water feature management, from lighting to water flow, into a single network that can be controlled remotely, enhancing operational efficiency. By staying ahead of these trends, pond and water feature businesses can position themselves as industry leaders with cutting-edge solutions that meet the changing needs of their clients and the market.

Pioneers of the Pond and Water Feature Industry

The water feature and pond industry has seen various innovators who have significantly contributed through pioneering designs, technologies, and sustainability practices. Let's explore a few notable examples and analyse what makes them stand out and how they can inspire today's entrepreneurs in the industry.

Peter Waddington - Innovation in Koi Pond Filtration

Peter Waddington pioneered the koi industry and is mainly known for his advancements in koi pond filtration systems. His approach focused on enhancing the quality of water to ensure the health and longevity of koi carp. Waddy was a very influential person in my life, a strong character at times but one that is still inspiring today. He is now credited in the history books as one of the original koi gods from the UK. Waddy's deep understanding of koi biology and fish farming requirements led him to develop tailored filtration solutions.

He was very active at the koi shows in the 90s and was willing to share knowledge; I so wish I could roll back the clock and re-listen to one of his classes. These talks helped spread his innovative methods and reinforced his reputation as an expert. Waddy's legacy highlights the importance of specialisation and the potential impact of becoming an authoritative voice in a niche area. His dedication to education and quality improvement helped to raise standards within the hobby and industry.

Evolution Aqua and K1 Filter Media

Evolution Aqua introduced K1 filter media from the wastewater industry and made a Moving Bed Filter that revolutionised biological filtration in water features. The K1 media is designed to provide increased surface area for beneficial bacteria to thrive, essential for breaking down ammonia and nitrites in pond systems. When I first heard and saw this filter media in the early 90s, I was amazed but sceptical as it couldn't be that good (after doing tests at college, I was sold). I still use this filter media today in my fish farming efforts.

The design of the K1 media allows it to move freely within a filter chamber, improving biological filtration efficiency. The system enhances the environmental sustainability of pond ecosystems by ensuring cleaner water with less maintenance. You can learn from Evolution Aqua's approach to product innovation, which meets customer needs and advances sustainability. Investing in research and development to offer superior products can set a business apart in competitive markets.

Aquascape Inc. - Leading Ecosystem-Based Pond Solutions

Aquascape Inc. has been very influential in my business, putting money into my pocket. Their approach is popularising ecosystem-based pond solutions and decorative water features. At first, they significantly impacted the North American market. After a decade of my support on this side of the big pond, they are gradually expanding this way. 2024 has seen them opening up into the UK, leading them to reach more of Europe. The Aquascape approach focuses on creating natural-looking water features that are easier to maintain and support the local ecosystem. Building ponds that work with nature rather than against it promotes sustainability and ease of maintenance.

I want to relate the Aquascape Ecosystem Pond to free-range conditions to create a beautiful water feature instead of wastewater management for intensively farming fish, which needs attention, as in the last two examples. The Aquascape approach inspires the solopreneur aquatic artist, offering a proven system combining aesthetics with ecological function. Their commitment to supporting small businesses through education and community-building initiatives shows how aligning with innovative and supportive partners can amplify growth and impact in new markets.

These examples have provided insight into leveraging expertise, embracing technological advancements, and focusing on sustainability to build a successful and influential brand. Each story represents a stride in garden water features and serves as a blueprint for integrating passion, innovation, and strategic thinking into business practices.

Becoming a Thought Leader

Establishing yourself as a thought leader is a powerful way to elevate your business profile and influence industry standards and practices. This section guides you on becoming a thought leader, leveraging your expertise to make a significant impact.

Regularly sharing insightful content can significantly increase your visibility in the industry. This enhanced recognition can lead to more business opportunities and partnerships. As a thought leader, you are positioned at the forefront of industry advancements. Sharing knowledgeable content establishes trust and credibility with your audience, including potential customers and peers. This reputation can be crucial in a competitive market.

To establish yourself as a thought leader in the field of garden water features, pond design, and maintenance, you can consider these actionable strategies:

1. Start writing articles about your expertise in gardening magazines, local news channels, or your website. Share your unique ideas, showcase your masterpieces, and highlight the latest trends in your field.

2. Seek opportunities to speak at industry conferences like Water Garden Expo, Pondemonium, or RHS shows. These platforms allow you to connect with other professionals and potential customers while sharing your knowledge and style of aquatic art.

3. Organise and send out invitations to workshops or mini-events where you can offer practical advice and training on the latest technologies or techniques in pond management. Depending on your preference and reach, you can conduct these events in person at pond parties or online.

In today's digital era, online platforms provide helpful tools for sharing knowledge and establishing thought leadership in any industry.

A few examples are:

- **Social media**

  Use LinkedIn, Twitter, and Facebook platforms to share insights and engage with followers. You can also participate in industry-related discussions, which helps maintain a consistent presence. Respond to your audience's comments, questions, and feedback, which will help build a community around your content and enhance your credibility.

- **Video content**

  Creating and sharing video content on platforms like YouTube, Facebook, or Instagram can be very effective. Customers enjoy watching videos demonstrating the before-and-after of successful projects. You can also invite collaboration with other content creators to showcase your work and thoughts. Video content broadens your network and introduces you to their audiences.

- **Podcasts**

  Consider starting your own podcast or speaking on existing industry podcasts. Discuss topics of interest to pond enthusiasts and professionals, offering advice and insights that listeners can apply to their water feature projects. Continuous learning ensures your content remains relevant and insightful, keeping your audience engaged.

Remember that your unique insights and experiences are valuable. By sharing your knowledge and expertise, you contribute to the pond industry's development and build a lasting legacy that transcends ordinary business achievements. Embrace this role with enthusiasm and a commitment to excellence, and watch as it transforms your business and professional life.

Developing a long-term vision is crucial for making strategic decisions. Your vision should be ambitious yet achievable, inspiring yet grounded in reality.

To refine your vision, follow these steps:

1. **Reflect on personal values**

   Consider what drives you personally and professionally. How can these values be integrated into your business's long-term goals? For example, if sustainability is a core value, how can you innovate to make your pond installations more eco-friendly?

2. **Understand market needs**

   Stay updated with emerging trends in the pond industry, from eco-conscious practices to technological advancements. Align your vision with these trends to ensure it remains relevant and compelling.

3. **Envision the future**

   Imagine where your business will be in 10 or 20 years. What kind of projects do you want to undertake? What reputation do you wish to have in the industry? This forward-thinking approach will help shape a robust vision guiding your business.

Strategic Future Growth

Strategic planning is crucial for the sustained growth of your pond business. Diversify your services, invest in technology, build strategic partnerships, and prepare for future scenarios. Remember that every step today sets the foundation for your business's future success, so think big, plan carefully, and act decisively.

As you craft your long-term vision and strategic plan, remember that these are not just forecasting exercises but vital tools for shaping your business's future. They require thoughtful consideration, a deep understanding of your market, and a commitment to your core values. Embrace this process with optimism and a proactive stance, leveraging your insights and strategies to adapt to and influence the pond industry's future trajectory.

In the dynamic field of pond design and water feature installation, continuous learning is not just beneficial—it's essential. You must commit to ongoing education and personal development to stay ahead of technological advancements, changing market trends, and evolving customer preferences.

Continuous learning is crucial for professionals in the garden water feature industry. By staying updated with the latest techniques, materials, and regulations, enhancing skills, and fostering innovation, professionals can ensure their business remains competitive and appealing to clients. Some recommended resources for professional development include attending industry conferences, pursuing certifications from recognised industry bodies, enrolling in online courses and webinars, and joining mastermind groups.

To cultivate a culture of innovation, professionals can schedule internal workshops and brainstorming sessions, allocate resources for experimentation, establish feedback loops, engage in scenario planning, develop flexible business models, and stay open to integrating new technologies. By investing in continuous learning and embracing a culture of innovation, professionals can shape the industry's future and ensure long-term success.

To ensure sustainable growth, balance short-term objectives with long-term goals. Prioritise flexibility, integrate milestones and regularly review and adjust your business's performance against your strategic plan.

Practical Exercise: Goal Setting for Success

1. **List your goals**

   Begin by setting aside some quiet time for reflection and brainstorming. Write down ten goals you aim to achieve within the next 12 months with a pen and paper. Phrase these goals in the present tense to affirm that you are already on the path to achieving them. For example:

   "I earn £50,000 profit from our pond installations."
   "I drive a reliable top-of-the-range work vehicle that supports my business needs."
   "I own the latest pond maintenance equipment."
   "I have saved £15,000 for our early buy and personal development."
   "I've set up a standing order to put aside £500 extra weekly for my pension."
   "I travel to multiple countries for work-related purposes."
   "I attract and support a dozen other professionals with my consultancy services."

2. **Identify the most impactful goal**

   Review your list and ask yourself which goal, when achieved, would have the most significant positive impact on your personal and professional life. This goal will be your primary focus.

3. **Break down the goal**

   Take your most impactful goal and break it down into smaller, manageable tasks. Create a list of every step you need to take to achieve this goal. For example, if your goal is to earn £50,000 from your pond installations:

   - Research the current market rates for garden ponds from top industry professionals.
   - Look at ways to reduce your overhead costs, as this will affect your profit margins.
   - Develop new aquatic art packages or premium pond offerings with a much higher profit margin.
   - Attract the best aquatic artists to your team, or be someone everyone wants.
   - Create a marketing plan to attract higher-paying clients.
   - Increase online presence to showcase work and gather testimonials.

4. **Organise and prioritise**

   Turn your list of tasks into a checklist. Arrange these tasks by priority and sequence, determining which steps should be completed first. Assign deadlines to each task to ensure steady progress towards your goal.

5. **Take action**

   It's essential to commit to taking daily action towards your goals. Even small daily steps will compound over time, leading to significant progress. Keep your checklist visible as a daily reminder of your objectives, and review your progress regularly. Every morning, take some time to review your goals and the tasks for that day. Each evening, reflect on the progress made and plan for the next day. Consistently putting in effort will help to turn your ambitions into habits, paving the way for you to achieve your long-term vision.

6. **Write a letter to your future self**

   For a more profound reflection, write a letter to your future self, describing what you have achieved in the future. This exercise can profoundly solidify your goals and the reasons behind them. You might write about your accomplishments in the next 12 months or extend it to 3 or 5 years. Describe the benefits and improvements these achievements have brought into your life.

For example:

"Dear Mark (Future Me),

Today is August 29th 2025 (one year from now), and I am happy to report that I have achieved my goal of earning £50,000 profit from my company's pond installations (please note I am not in the hole or sales office). This achievement allowed me to reinvest in my business, enhance the tools, and expand our offerings. I feel proud and confident, knowing our hard work has paid off and the team is happy to be recognised as the leading pond-building professionals in the Midlands. My focus, leadership commitment, and daily efforts have made this possible."

These steps will set a solid foundation for your business's growth and personal development, turning your ambitions into achievable targets.

Money is a resource; it will come and go, which is different from the other two resources we all have: Time and Energy. Be careful how you use it.

12

CREATING A BUSINESS THAT MATTERS

This section focuses on the transformative power of water feature businesses in achieving personal satisfaction and success and making a meaningful impact on the community. It examines how aligning your business with deeply held values and desires for happiness can create lasting benefits for yourself and those around you.

The Pursuit of Happiness in Business

Start by asking yourself, "I am happy when...?"

If you find yourself in a spot, reflecting on this question can help you align your business activities with what genuinely brings you joy and fulfilment.

Happiness often stems from simplicity—pain-free, comfortable, and well-cared-for, like infancy. In adult life, especially in business, this translates into pursuing rewarding and enriching work rather than merely profitable work.

Personal Fulfilment
Evaluate whether your business activities make you feel like you're just enriching someone else or are a true expression of your dreams. If your daily work isn't contributing to your happiness, it might be time to rethink your goals and the projects you undertake.

Project Focus
Avoid winging it. Detailed planning and breaking down your dreams into achievable projects can significantly enhance your chances of success. This approach ensures you are not just dreaming but actively creating memories and impactful experiences through your work.

Enhancing Community Well-Being Through Your Business

Water feature businesses possess a unique capacity to enhance community spaces, making them more vibrant and ecologically friendly. Integrating your business activities with community enhancement projects enriches your surroundings and forges deeper connections with local people and other businesses.

Living the Water Gardening Lifestyle
Start by embodying the values you want to promote. If water gardening enhances your personal life by bringing peace and beauty into your daily routine, use your business as a platform to spread these benefits to others.

Core Values in Action
Implement core values focusing on meaningful work with and for people who matter. This could involve enhancing local spaces with beautiful water features, contributing to local wildlife habitats, or helping beautify communal spaces, which can foster a more vital community spirit—doing things that matter, with people that matter, for people that matter.

The Sawyer Mason Foundation's "Inspiring Love for Nature" offers a fantastic example of how water feature businesses can use their skills for community benefit. If you charge what you are worth, you can free up time, money, and energy, but make sure you have nutrition first. You can only do something or help others if you have nutrition. It's incredible how you can significantly improve public areas and contribute positively to local ecosystems by volunteering your time and resources.

An example project by the Sawyer Mason Foundation highlights the therapeutic impact of water features in a community setting. The foundation gifted a therapeutic water garden to Nikki, a military veteran whose career was cut short by a severe car accident. During her recovery, Nikki found comfort and healing in the peacefulness of waterfalls and rivers. The foundation's water feature became her home retreat, aiding her recovery and enhancing her mental well-being.

This demonstrated the potential of water features as havens for healing and contemplation. John G Adams, the grandfather of Sawyer Mason Adams, for whom the foundation is named, turned pain into purpose after hearing about others who had lost someone while caring for others.

Business and Community Development
Participating in charitable efforts like those of the Sawyer Mason Foundation can significantly raise a business' profile and strengthen bonds within the community. Volunteering demonstrates a commitment to community well-being and can lead to more business opportunities through increased visibility and public goodwill. These activities benefit the community and enhance the business's image, making it a valued part of the local environment. This shared growth supports business

success and community enhancement, creating a lasting impact beyond commercial benefits.

By focusing on activities that align with personal values of happiness and community service, water feature professionals can achieve greater satisfaction and success, creating a positive impact that resonates beyond the confines of traditional business metrics.

Your business should not just achieve financial success; it should positively impact your family and enrich your clients' lives.

Leaving a Legacy Through Your Work

Think about the legacy you want to leave, and let's start with the end in mind. How do you want to lead your life? Are you looking to lead a large team, or would you prefer creating art with a small, quick and nimble operation? Do you envision working a few days a week, or are you committed to extensive, hands-on involvement?

Focus on Your Actual Value
Let's dig into this. When considering what type of water feature business to start or whether to change your current business, you must balance three key factors:

what you enjoy, what you're good at, and what can bring you significant financial rewards.

Many people fall into the trap of considering only one of these factors:

Passion Killer
Choosing a job just because you love it might sound ideal, but if it only pays minimum wage, you might soon start resenting what you once loved.

Comfort Zone
You might be good at something and make it your profession, but you'll burn out quickly if it's all work and no payoff.

It's All About the Money
A well-paying job might seem attractive, but not if it makes you miserable daily.

To truly thrive, *you must find a role that overlaps all three areas.* Instead of fitting yourself into a predetermined business model, identify your "value"—where your passions, skills, and potential for profit align—and then find the business opportunity that matches them.

Managing Your Resources: Time, Money, Energy

- List your activities: Write down everything you do, covering all aspects of your life.
- Let's now visualise how you allocate your time, money and energy across these activities listed.

Suppose you had 100 buttons for each resource, each with a different but the same colour.
100 Time Buttons = How much time is spent monthly on each activity?
100 Money Buttons = What is the proportion of your monthly spending per segment?
100 Energy Buttons = These indicate the energy each task requires of you.

As you can see, each set of 100 buttons equals your monthly amount. I want you to allocate your buttons to each segment now. If you do not have 300 physical buttons, write a number or use different colours to represent each activity. Please stay within 100 for each resource. Other ways are okay; whatever works for you, it needs to be a way to tell quickly, from a glance.

Now you know where your resources are going. Remember, you might find ways to increase your money, but time and energy are finite resources. Be careful where you allocate it.

Are you happy with how your resources are being allocated? This exercise is interesting because you have the resources and can choose where to allocate them.

When building a business, especially at the start, it's vital to dedicate yourself fully without getting distracted by other opportunities. This intense focus is necessary because even a tiny distraction could derail your progress when resources are limited.

Consider maintaining a journal or blog to document your journey, documenting where your resource buttons are getting spent, your work's influence, and your evolving thoughts about the future. This practice can enhance self-awareness and strategic thinking, enriching your life and business.

Let's Look at the End Game
If I took the finish line away, would you continue running?

Would you keep going if no one wanted to run with you or was cheering you on?

I don't want to stop running. I can't stop running.

From one of my favourite songs, 'Time' by Pink Floyd.

"One day, you find ten years have got behind you. No one told you when to run; you missed the starting gun."

Later in the song is another line that fits in with this last section.

"Hanging on in quiet desperation is the English way."

Time is all we have, and you can't get it back. So, let's start running together in the right direction, thinking about what's next.

This section serves as a comprehensive guide to thinking strategically about a business from the outset, not just as a venture to manage day-to-day but as an asset that might be transitioned. If you're a solopreneur which is deeply involved and wearing all the hats in all aspects of your business, you may need guidance on approaching potential growth and scaling challenges.

You may find yourself contemplating your next steps. Are you considering selling your business, transferring ownership to a family member, or scaling back to a part-time involvement? Careful consideration and planning are essential to ensure that the transition is smooth and successful.

As a business owner, it's essential to take a moment to reflect on the reasons that drove you to start your business in the first place. It may be your passion for ponds, love for working outdoors, or commitment to conservation. Whatever your foundational motivations were, you must keep them at the forefront when making decisions and formulating business strategies. By doing so, you'll stay true to your original vision and achieve personal fulfilment through your work.

If you plan to sell, transfer, or scale down your business, taking practical steps to ensure its continued success is essential. If now is the time, you should get your business professionally valued to understand its worth. Businesses are only worth something if you can remove the owner and it still functions. If the business is of value, you should ensure your business documentation is current, including contracts, financial records, and operational procedures.

Consider your future role, if any, and how it aligns with your personal goals and lifestyle changes.

If you plan to transfer your business to a family member or sell it to an outside buyer, plan a comprehensive training and handover period to ensure a smooth transition. Create a handover document that includes insights into daily operations, key contacts and business nuances that only you might know. It's vital to seek legal and financial advice to ensure that all aspects of the business transition are legally sound and financially wise.

Reflect on your initial motivations and align them with your plans. Aligning these goals with the new business strategy is essential for personal and professional fulfilment. Ensure your goals are in line with the company's goals.

By taking these steps, you can help ensure that your business continues to thrive, whether under your watchful eye or that of a successor. You can also secure your legacy and achieve a sense of personal fulfilment.

Envision a future where you can still engage with your passion on a different scale. It may involve mentoring the next generation, focusing on select passion projects, or simply enjoying the environment they've helped shape.

Finally, consider whether you'd rather slow down rather than stop. Can you remain active in the industry at a less intensive pace—consulting, writing, or speaking at events? Will this fulfil your need for professional engagement without the demands of full-time business management?

Ask yourself this or finish this line, "I'm happy when?" What truly brings you joy and satisfaction in your personal and professional lives? When are you truly happy?

CONCLUSION
YOUR ROADMAP TO SUCCESS

You might have begun this book as someone curious about starting a business, looking to become self-employed, or as a seasoned entrepreneur seeking growth. Wherever you started, the destination involves crafting a company (or your perfect role) that thrives financially and enriches your life and community. A life without problems is boring, the opposite of happiness. Will you seize the day with the challenge and make your mark in the world of water features?

Throughout this book, we've explored the intricacies of building a sustainable water feature business—from the initial sparks of desire and passion to the complexities of business operations and customer relationships.

We've discussed practical steps for ensuring your business thrives through transitions, such as accurately valuing your business, updating crucial documentation, and planning comprehensively for succession or sale. We've also highlighted the importance of maintaining foundational motivations throughout these transitions, ensuring that your business reflects your values and visions.

You've learned the nuts and bolts of business. But more importantly, building a business or creating that perfect role is more than an income; it's about creating a legacy that impacts lives through your work and creativity.

Here are some of the critical takeaways from each part of the book:

Part 1: Foundations of Success
To attain success, it is imperative to clearly define your understanding of success, establish attainable objectives and formulate a comprehensive plan to accomplish them. Embracing a mindset that combines performance, passion, and purpose can be fulfilling, as can striving for resilience and continual learning. Sustainable practices benefit the environment, meet rising consumer expectations and can help navigate obstacles, positioning businesses for long-term success.

Part 2: Crafting Your Unique Offer

Balancing creativity and technical skills is essential in water feature design and construction. Finding your niche with signature designs is also necessary, whether it's still-water wildlife, formal architecture, ecosystem, or free-range koi pond designs. Considering dedicated fish pools is also crucial, as these styles are different, and you can't master all of them.

Part 3: Growing Your Business

Effective business and personal branding go beyond mere promotion; they involve embedding your unique identity into every aspect of your business, resonating with clients, and building lasting relationships. Your brand includes the art of selling and relationship building. Streamlined operations and proficient project management are crucial for maintaining efficiency and client satisfaction from inception to completion.

Part 4: Maximising Profit and Impact

Conducting a comprehensive business audit to assess your financial situation is critical. This involves appropriately pricing your services, exploring diverse revenue streams such as complementary services or strategic partnerships, and understanding the fear of letting go to enhance profitability significantly. Examining the challenges of business expansion and ways to incorporate innovations in your business model can open new markets and improve your financial stability.

Part 5: Building a Legacy
To position yourself as a thought leader, stay ahead of industry trends, engage in practical exercises for goal setting and strategic future growth, and develop unique offerings such as rentable features. This proactive approach fuels business innovation and ensures that your operations contribute positively to community and environmental sustainability, thus cementing a lasting legacy.

Now, we find ourselves flowing like water through a pipe; we hit a tee piece, and there are two closed ball valves, a blue one and a red one. Two paths starkly represent the decision; you only get to open one of the valves. The choice is yours, and it's a powerful one.

The blue valve opens a short path, letting you return to comfort, where no action is required. If that's the path you want, then enjoy. I wish you well.

The red valve opens a path that challenges you to push beyond the ordinary, strive for extraordinary achievements, and transform your passion into tangible success. As you have guessed, I love this red valve because it's always new and exciting, and the blue one gets dull. Sometimes, this red path will be variable, at times swift and noisy, and at others slow and quiet. Choose this path that leads you to a lasting impact on the world.

As we finish this journey, consider starting a new one. Remember that the heaviest weight in the gym isn't the barbell—it's the front door. I would be a fool if I thought you still didn't know it would be hard; it *will* get tough. The real challenge is your resilience—how you withstand and rise from the inevitable setbacks, unphased by the impacts that once might have deterred you.

Get back up; you will soon be able to look back, laugh, and enjoy the journey. Remember, cautionary thoughts will always be present, aiming to protect you. Yet, if you choose to take the challenging path—akin to opting for stairs over an elevator—strive to do it efficiently, keeping pace with or surpassing the more accessible routes. Work smarter, not harder.

Wherever you are in your journey, having a plan makes it much easier to move forward. What you do next is crucial, especially if you still need to take the time to reflect and set clear goals. Now is the perfect moment to pause, consider your current position, and thoughtfully plan your future direction. Dream, Plan, and Enjoy — this process is essential for success!

I have intentionally written this book to provide guidance and outline critical points. Each chapter builds on the last, so you can re-evaluate and reread parts anytime.

As you move forward, remember that the journey of entrepreneurship is continuous. There is always room for improvement, innovation, and growth.

Remember why you started as you ponder your next steps—selling your business, scaling back, or expanding. Was it a love for working and creating, a passion for the ponds, or a commitment to sustainability? Sometimes, you find yourself on the wrong path or have been hitting the easy button for too long. This book has given you the tools to find the right plan, a well-structured plan that will help you know what to do and where to go.

When you have a healthy business, and your cup is overflowing with joy, you can share the love and improve the world, bringing the love of nature to people. Writing this book taught me that business is accessible, but the implementation is challenging. You will have employee issues, customer issues, and mental battles. Still, it's all worth it when you see the people around you change and step up, the client's face when you hand over your beloved aquatic art, and the feeling you get when you and your family start living the water gardening lifestyle. Keep these drivers at the forefront as you plan your future moves.

Your journey begins now. With each step you take, strategy you implement, and the design you create, you build something remarkable for yourself, your community, and the future. Let the ripples you create today turn into waves of success and satisfaction.

Hopefully, this book has answered all your questions. But if you would like continued guidance, you can access additional resources that complement the content at https://mark.thepondadvisor.co.uk/business.html

We also have various in-person and digital companion services, from quick lunch and learn sessions that spark motivation to my comprehensive year-long mentorship programs offering ongoing support and advanced business insights. Each service is designed to enhance your learning and application of the book's content and is tailored to fit different stages of your business journey.

Remember, the world of garden water features isn't just about ponds and plants; it's about creating custom places for your customers every day, crafting beauty that endures, and building legacies that ripple through time. Grab that foam gun, burst through that door, and let's turn these ripples into waves and go and do something that's never been done before.

www.ingramcontent.com/pod-product-compliance
Lightning Source LLC
Chambersburg PA
CBHW070731020526
44118CB00035B/1170